RETURN TO
MAIN STREET

Nancy Eberle

RETURN TO MAIN STREET

A Journey to Another America

W·W·NORTON & COMPANY

New York   *London*

Published simultaneously in Canada by George J. McLeod Limited,
Toronto.

Printed in the United States of America

All Rights Reserved

First Edition

Library of Congress Cataloging in Publication Data
Eberle, Nancy.
  Return to main street.
    1. United States—Social conditions—1960–
  2. Urban-rural migration—United States. 3. Res
  idential mobility—United States. I. Title.
  HN59.E23 1982 304.8'2 81–9448
  ISBN 0–393–01485–1 AACR2

W. W. Norton & Company, Inc. 500 Fifth Avenue, New York, N.Y. 10110
W. W. Norton & Company Ltd. 37 Great Russelll Street, London, W.C. 1

1 2 3 4 5 6 7 8 9 0

For Dick
and for Jeannette

Contents

Acknowledgments

My thanks to Lynn and George Koons, who provided a quiet and comfortable place to work; to the Ragdale Foundation, which did the same; to William J. Petersen, author of *Steamboating on the Upper Mississippi*, for the stories of Daniel Harris and Moses Meeker; to my husband, Richard Eberle, for the generosity of spirit that made this book possible; and to the people of Galena, for sharing their stories and their lives. One of them, upon learning that I was writing a book about small-town life, said jokingly, "Are you going to tell the truth?" The answer is that it is my truth. There are undoubtedly other Galenas. This one is mine.

Introduction

"You're the third couple I've met in the last month who are moving to the country," said Ruth, the real estate agent, scowling and setting a glass of white wine on the patio table. "What's going on?"

We had met to set a price on the three-story Victorian in Evanston, Illinois where Dick and I had lived for four years. The price we set—$126,000—would buy the new owners thirteen rooms, three fireplaces, a big back yard, a tire swing hanging from a maple tree, and access to the amenities of a town known far and wide for its "quality of life."

What it would buy us was 150 miles away: two hundred acres bounded on two sides by a meandering river that led to the Mississippi, and the utterly transforming experience of belonging to a small town.

What was—and is—going on, although we didn't know it at the time, is that for the first time in the history of this nation since the westward expansion, more people are moving *from* the city *to* the country than the other way around, a fact quite as astonishing as if thousands of iron filings being drawn irrevocably toward a magnet suddenly reversed their direction.

The statistics tell the story. In the sixties, metropolitan areas showed a gain of almost six million and nonmetropolitan areas showed a loss of almost three million— both through migration.* Between 1970 and 1978 however, the influx to metropolitan areas had slowed to a mere trickle—566,000, spread out over 288 metropolitan

---

*The discrepancy is accounted for by international migration.

areas ranging from New York City to Billings, Montana. Meanwhile, the rural areas had not only stemmed the outgoing tide, but had picked up 2,875,000 people. Rural counties were gaining people in the seventies as fast as they were losing them in the sixties!*

The move to the country that these figures bear witness to is not merely a move down the road a piece to the last stop on the 6:17. It is a move out beyond the city's ganglia—beyond reach of its commuter trains, beyond the circulation area of its newspapers, beyond the signals of its television stations, and beyond the billboard blandishments of its commercial establishments.

Though in our case moving to the country meant moving to a farm (a farm from which we can clearly see the small town that is the true center of our new lives), this is the exception rather than the rule. Farms are generally too expensive, too demanding, and just too strange and unfamiliar to appeal to many. Neither does the current move to the country mean the remote log cabin in the woods or the tepee in the pasture of the sixties.

Today's transplants (and those who are biding their time until the circumstances in their own lives are right for departure) are far more likely to choose a pretty little town surrounded by green space—a town that is not a suburb or an exurb but its own self with a character as strong as an individual's, a town where the air is fresh and you can hear the birds and you can walk anywhere and no one ever asks for identification. Or, alternatively,

---

*The term "metropolitan area," as used by the U.S. Census Department from which these figures are taken, is, roughly speaking, any county with a city of fifty thousand in it plus all counties feeding a high proportion of commuters to that city. The Chicago metropolitan area, for example, consists of six counties. In fact, the formula is a complicated one that admits the inclusion of cities even smaller than fifty thousand as the nexus of a metropolitan area in low-population states, with the result that when the Census talks of *non*-metropolitan areas they are talking about the real boonies.

they seek five or ten acres outside of such a town where they can have a vegetable garden, and perhaps keep a few chickens and maybe a goat as a pet for the children. If those who are moving to the country today have a somewhat different dream than those who left in the sixties, it may be because they are somewhat different people. The biggest mistake anyone can make about the phenomenon is to toss it off as something which involves only the rich, the retired, or the radical. The new pioneers, like those of long ago, are a heterogenous group. Since moving to the country I have met—and you will meet some of them in these pages—people whose previous occupations were salesman, seamstress, broker, electrician, journalist, lawyer, restaurant manager, medical technician, systems analyst, caseworker, manufacturer, and liquor store owner, to name but a few. Some are members of traditional families, some are childless couples, some are single parents, and some have never been married. Some are clearly adventurous souls; a far greater number are utterly conventional. What distinguishes them is that they have begun that process which all social critics agree must take place if we are to survive our own technology: the process of choosing which of the world's baggage they will take with them. The people I know are anything but doctrinaire in their choices. They grow their own vegetables in chemical-free gardens, but cook them in microwave ovens. They hang their wash on a clothesline between April and October, but dry it in an automatic dryer between October and April.

Why do they come to the country? To live closer to the natural world—the world of trees and rivers and rocks and lakes and woods and fields and wildlife that is, after all, our ultimate home; to escape pollution, crime, traffic, noise, indifference, rudeness, regimentation, high prices and low returns; to lead a life less focused on getting and having—free from the "Buy! Buy! Buy!" drummed at the consciousness from every quarter like the sound of someone else's radio on the subway; to live a shared life, husband and wife, parents and children, where intimacy is not an epiphany but grows out of common experience; and finally, to lead a simpler, more integrated life. Can the country provide these things? The answer, from this admittedly partisan corner, is a resounding yes. But the country provides something else as well—something so long-forgotten that it is not even missed: a sense of community.

In *Human Scale,* his breakthrough book about the devastating effects of the "bigger is better" philosophy on our planet, Kirkpatrick Sale points out that the community is a far, far older institution than the family, and the instinct for community is as powerful as the instinct for sex, "since the former appears as necessary for survival as the latter is for procreation."

Obviously not all constellations of human beings constitute a community, and Sale finds the suburbs and all but an occasional urban neighborhood singularly wanting in community cohesion. The hallmarks of community, he says, are regular associations between people, easy access to public officers, mutual aid among neighbors, and open and trusting social relations. Smallness, he argues, is simply essential to preserving intimacy, trust, honesty, mutuality, cooperation, democracy, and congeniality.

But what is a congenial size for a community? Drawing upon disciplines from biology to anthropology to urban planning, and on the record of human communities from prehistoric times to the present, Sale finds an astonishing measure of agreement as to the answer. There are two magic numbers in human society—500 and 5,000. The first is the neighborhood, actually consisting of 400 to 1,000 people (500 is the optimum). The second is the community, made up of 5,000 to 10,000 (5,000 being the optimum). The fact that humankind everywhere on the globe and throughout the course of history has solved the problems of collective living at these levels suggests that they deserve our consideration.

Happily, they are getting it today. The popularity of country music, wood stoves, L.L. Bean, antiques, natural foods, prefab log cabins, home gardens, and *Mother Earth News* (whose circulation is now an astonishing one million, 50 percent of it in urban centers) would suggest to even the slowest a fascination with "country." But it is far more than that. When the precipitous drops in the populations of big cities make headline news, when the number of those moving to rural areas is significant enough for the USDA to dedicate its yearbook, as it did in 1978, to those *Living on a Few Acres,* when the Stanford Institute suggests that the trend of the eighties is likely to be "voluntary simplicity" accompanied by decentralization, when not only individuals but industries are moving to small towns, when the growth rate of rural areas is twice that of cities, it's time to sit up and take notice.

The reversal of America's traditional migration pattern has profound implications for our national life, but examining them is not our purpose here. It is, rather, to describe one tiny fragment (population 3,876) of another America, an America far, far different from the urban/-suburban one, and an America that is vast and real and available to those who seek it. It is also the story of one family that left the suburbs for the country—why we did it, what we found when we got there, and what it has meant to our lives.

Nancy Eberle

Galena, Illinois

RETURN TO
MAIN STREET

"It was a lively little town. The houses were none of them painted, but there was that snap about the place which gave promise of great things in the future."

Traveler to Galena, 1829

"We saw a river, and a little red brick town, and houses on a hill. It was late afternoon, and beautiful and golden. The next day we put a bid on a house, and went back to San Francisco. Six weeks later we moved in."

Jim Hirsheimer, 1979

Main Street

Picture a primitive.

Left foreground, a Victorian railroad station, ferns in baskets hanging from its windows, twin white cupolas rising from its roof. Right foreground, a white gazebo atop a mound of green, redolent of band concerts on summer nights. In the middle ground, curling like ribbons across the canvas, a penny-green river and a red brick town. Above the town, shuttered houses and white-steepled churches levitate through the green until they reach an azure sky where puffy white clouds redress the balance.

Now move closer, until peripheral vision is gone.

That's Main Street—there, through those floodgates. They call those old brick buildings on either side of it "The Wall." Most of them were built in the 1850s when everyone thought this was going to be the New Orleans of the Upper Mississippi. Makes you feel like you've stepped back into another century, doesn't it? That's what people generally notice first about the town—its age. That and its beauty. Then they see that it's getting pretty shabby and rundown in places. And finally they realize that they're seeing something *real*—something that wasn't created just for them. You'd think city people moving in might spoil that—you know, make it into one of those places that look like they were done by a set designer and where all the stores are called "shoppes." But they haven't. It's partly because the town's stubborn. But there's something else. The people who are moving in don't want plastic and cute. They've had enough. The way the town is, is why they're here.

That's Jim Hirsheimer—that fellow in the red brick warehouse writing price tags on the antiques he's picked up over the weekend. Jim and his wife came here from California on their honeymoon, looking for a good place to live. They drove from town to town in a Winnebago and when they saw this—well, that was it. There's a lot of folks like the Hirsheimers here. That woman in the red car who waved at us is Kathy Webster. She grew up in a small town and swore she'd never go back. Now she says she'd never go back to the city. Kathy's on the school board.

Let me show you around a bit. That big orange brick building with its windows gaping is the hotel—or used to be. Folks are pretty upset about it. You'll hear the story later. And over there, under the sign that says "EAT" is the Steakburger Inn. It's a good place for homemade pie and the coffee's only a dime a cup. Nice folks, too. Across the street's the Ben Franklin. That's Mr. Jividen, rolling down the awning so that the sun won't fade the things in the window. And that's Mrs. Jividen, helping that little girl choose a birthday gift for her mother. The kitchens and closets and dresser drawers of Galena are filled with Mrs. Jividen's choices. Calendar dish towels. Pearl earrings. Dusting powder. Knick-knacks.

See the sign on that storefront window that says "Vincent, Roth and Elliott"? Dick Elliott's another one. He used to be a labor lawyer for Quaker Oats. There's not much need for a labor lawyer around here. All we've got is the two foundries and the cheese factory, and all three payrolls don't add up to 200 people. But there's plenty of legal work to do. People divorce and die and go bankrupt here just like anywhere else. Besides, it's the county seat. There's not much crime—perhaps a dozen arrests in a week for "excessive acceleration" or "loitering in a dram shop" and things of that nature. For that matter, there's not even a stoplight in town. In fact, there's not a single stoplight in all six hundred square miles of Jo Daviess County. "Last county in Illinois without a stoplight"— that's what the nurse up at the hospital told me. No parking meters, either. When you come right down to it, there aren't many people: 3,876 in Galena, and 22,390 in the county. What does that come to? Three per square mile?

We're holding our own, though. Small towns are beginning to look awfully good to people. All kinds of people. You know, there are a lot of jobs today that let you live anywhere. There's a fellow here who designs blast furnaces, for example, and another who's a maritime lawyer. What difference does it make to them where they live? As far as their jobs go, that is. But from the other point of view it makes a whole lot of difference.

People come here because life is simpler here, but you know why they stay? Because it's happier. When you go to the bank or the grocery store or the drugstore, people call you by name and say, "How's it going?" When you go to see the dentist, instead of lying in the chair and staring at the squares in the ceiling and worrying about your kids or your job or your marriage, he's telling you about his garden or you're telling him about yours, because he isn't "The Dentist." He's someone you know. It's the same way everywhere here.

And look around. I've noticed people almost never say, "I came here because it's beautiful." It's as if they were embarrassed by it. But people do care. Who wants to live in a place where the only trees are those spindly little things with wires to hold them up? Look at that sky and those hills. Here, let's go up to Prospect Street where we have a better view. Takes your breath away, doesn't it? Sometimes I'll stop here on my way home and just sit and look for a while. Even after two years, I can hardly believe it's real.

That steeple down there is First Presbyterian. That one's the Methodist. That's Saint Michael's and that's Westminster Presbyterian. There's a couple more behind us. All the churches in town get together for Bible school each summer. One year when the text was "Joshua and the Battle of Jericho" the kids marched all over the town and ended up at the levee and tried to blow it down with paper trumpets. I would love to have seen that.

That mound on your left is Horseshoe Mound. Billy White's family has owned most of it for six generations. Lost it once and got it back. When you stand up there and look out over the Mississippi it's like seeing it out the window of an airplane, only you can feel the wind and smell it and it smells like hay.

The mound in the middle is Dygerts. All these mounds are natural, made of something called churt that doesn't wear down, even after millions of years. We have the other kind, too—Indian mounds. Some anthropologists came up here back in the twenties and found thirty of them on my neighbor's farm. Inside the mounds were tombs made of log and rock, and inside the tombs were skeletons and pots and even some pearls. Probably Mississippi River pearls. I found one once, in a clam, about as big as those tiny beads that the Indians used to decorate their clothes with. I know pearls come from oysters as well as you do, but this was a clam and it was a pearl. The mound on the right is Pilot Knob. It's called that because in the old days they lit fires up there for the Mississippi River pilots so they'd know the entrance to the Galena River was coming up. It's hard to believe, but that little river down there used to be almost three hundred feet wide and seventy feet deep—deeper than the Mississippi. You could sit on the banks and watch the steamboats go by all day. What for? Why, for lead! That's what Galena means—lead. The mines around here produced almost all of the country's lead right before the Civil War. America's very first boom town. What happened? That's another story. This old town is full of stories—stories of steamboat captains and Civil War generals and miners and murderers. The new people have stories, too. Chasing a dream is still a grand adventure, even if you're traveling in a U-Haul instead of a covered wagon.

Our place is over that way, toward the Mississippi. You can't see it from here. You can't see it from the road, either, unless you know exactly where to look, because it's a mile back in. You have to drive through a pasture, then around some gullies and then go through a cornfield, and when you come out of the cornfield, you're starting up the hill. It's a terrible hill. We couldn't get up it for days at a time that first winter. Anyway, when you get to the top you're there.

When we came here from the city two years ago we didn't know anything about any of this. The town was just a place to stop late Friday night to pick up some bread and milk for the weekend. It's like Dick Elliott said: "Everyone thinks they're the first."

PART ONE

Seeking

It is as hard to trace the seeds of dissatisfaction that lead to change in an individual life as it is to trace the origins of a social movement. Looking back, I think ours were planted on the windowsill of a Chicago brownstone five years before we came here. It was a tall, deep-set, south-facing window, ideal for growing plants, and like so many other urban couples that year we spent our Saturdays shopping the moist and steamy environments of plant boutiques with names like "The Fertile Delta."

As fall gave way to winter, our plant population spilled from windowsill to floor, climbed from floor to table, and from table to macrame hangers suspended from the ceiling. With spring, the plants were unceremoniously dispatched from the windowsill, and flats of seeds covered in Glad Wrap took their place. That was the year our landlord told us we could have the four-by-six plot of earth outside our window for a garden. But he was too late; shortly later, we left for the suburbs. Harry, the oldest of our three sons, was ready for high school, and in one of the paradoxes of city living, the school serving the best neighborhood in the city was the worst school in the city, a school whose very name raised the hairs on the back of the neck and sent parents who had stuck out eight years of public education for better or for worse scurrying for scholarships to Francis Parker or The Latin School.

Far from fleeing the city, however, we left with mixed emotions and chose the least suburban of Chicago's suburbs: Evanston, a bastion of interracial living on Chicago's North Shore, home of Northwestern University, and a city in its own right with a population of eighty thousand.

We fell in love with the kind of house the town is known for: a big old Victorian with original woodwork and stained glass, nooks and crannies, three fireplaces and three floors, and a big backyard. On the day we first saw it there was a barber pole in the center hall, an icebox in the living room, and a jukebox in the kitchen. I think the irreverence of the former owners was as persuasive as its intrinsic beauty. On the day that we moved in we found a note on the fireplace mantel that was like a benediction: "Take care of this wonderful old house and it will take care of you"—followed by pages of phone numbers and notes on how to coax the washer along and where to buy the *Sunday New York Times*.

No sooner had we put the boxes away than Dick began digging a garden. When he was finished, all that remained of the backyard was a ten-foot band of grass beside the back door. We planted everything we knew and loved and things we'd never tasted. When we weren't working in the garden, we were working inside, painting tiger lilies and geraniums across the old metal kitchen cabinets, tearing down walls and putting up new ones.

The boys were happy in the schools which seemed so excellent to us that we were surprised when other parents found anything to criticize. In fact, the entire quality of life in Evanston was awesome: city employees in little dune buggies cruising the streets in search of Dutch Elm disease; playgrounds for children with the newest, most imaginative equipment at virtually every corner; a library so busy that a week's grace on overdue books was automatic; miles of bicycle paths and beaches along the lake; special buses for the elderly that would take them to any doorstep in the city; and all the resources of a major university.

Every need was anticipated. Did you yearn to ice-skate in August? The multimillion-dollar Crown Center was ready and waiting with not one, but several rinks. Did you want your children to learn tennis? Sign them up with the city recreation department. Did you yourself hanker to write a novel, learn Russian, or do your own wiring? The schools were as busy with adults at night as with children during the day. Commuters didn't even need to take a train: Chicago's El made five stops in Evanston—express service to the heart of the city at any hour of the day for fifty cents. It was, very simply, the best: the greenery of suburban living without loss of cosmopolitanism; excellent interracial schools without busing; good commuting without undue expense.

If the town offered all that anyone could want, so, it seemed, did our own lives. Though we had scraped to make the down payment on the house, our income had steadily increased and we were relatively free of financial worry. We liked our jobs, Dick as a commodity trader on the Chicago Board of Trade, and I as a vice-president of the Chicago Board Options Exchange. If Dick's job veered between the harrowing and the boring, it nevertheless offered an independence more often associated with the arts than the world of finance. He was his own boss, without burden of overhead, employees, or payroll. If my job was sometimes exhausting and sometimes frustrating, it was nevertheless fulfilling, and had plenty of flash besides. We traveled, not widely or often, but enough to refresh: a business trip to New York, a houseboat trip on the Mississippi, a vacation in Florida.

To the pleasure we took in the three boys was added the total enchantment and fascination of a new baby daughter. I quit my job, and though the transition was not easy, I was soon as absorbed by writing as I had been by explaining the intricacies of the option market to press and public. We were forever launching a project or discovering a passion. We built a deck. We raised bees. We fell in and out of love with Oriental rugs and salt-water aquariums. We went to movies. We read. We bicycled in the moonlight. We gardened. And we loved each other.

I can't remember when our disenchantment began. Perhaps we were never enchanted, only busy. Or perhaps busyness is a form of enchantment, delaying or obscuring entirely the perception of what is real and essential. I do remember that at night, when the dishes were done and Kate put to bed, there came to be a listless, empty feeling to the hours ahead, an emptiness too often filled with the television we had once consigned to a closet.

I remember a house gone dead with respect, its rooms like the galleries of a museum, until we had begun to live in the kitchen, like immigrants in the back of the shop.

I remember being embarrassed by the awful predictability, the stupidity of my conversations with the children—"How was school?" . . . "Have you done your homework?"—but being unable to think of anything else to say.

I remember beginning to prefer green and sun-splashed restaurants to dark, intime ones.

I remember the curious feeling of oppression that came over me each week as I read the *Evanston Review,* which may be the only paper in the country that gave its first half-dozen pages over to "Arts and Amusements". There were plenty of both in town: plays, galleries, concerts, lectures, films. I would dutifully circle those events that might be fun, rip out the pages and stick them to the refrigerator with a magnet. But they had all the attraction of the canned tomato display at Dominick's. Too much choice, in any area of life, has a paralyzing effect.

I remember getting increasingly angry at lines at checkout counters, librarians who didn't recognize me, indifferent sales clerks, traffic directives like "You MUST turn right," and alternate-side-of-the-street parking. Dick had his own list of aggravations: beach tokens, building permits, one-way streets, two-month waits for dental appointments.

There was also something vaguely disturbing about Evanston's largesse, which admittedly flowed to rich and poor alike. How many playgrounds can the children of a town utilize? Does a sunken street curb call for a new one, with new sod trucked in and regular watering by city employees? Does a high school need a greenhouse, five libraries, and four resource centers? Even the children were offended when, for the national bicentennial, the town decided to build itself a new fountain.

I have no answer to those who would say, and did, "Well, why *not?* What harm in it?" I can only say that it gave a feeling of unreality to our lives, as if we were all characters in someone else's play.

Finally, I remember Dick standing in the backyard, his feet planted between the cauliflower and the broccoli, his arms akimbo, his palms outstretched, saying, "I need . . . *more.*" We did not know what was wrong, but we were soon to get a glimmer of what was right.

It has always been hard for me to evaluate how tough

I am—a term of approval in our family. Compared to lone women ranchers, skydivers, and cleaning women who work all night in empty offices to send their children to college, I'm pretty soft. On the other hand, I tend to agree to a lot of things that friends of the same age and state in life shun as the sheerest sort of insanity. Like *driving* to Central America with two pouting teenagers (Harry, the oldest, had wisely decided to join us later), a twelve-month-old baby, four hundred Pampers, a portacrib, two 10-speed bicycles, a collapsible boat, a 35-hp motor, and a typewriter. (I may not be tough, but I am unfailingly optimistic.) We had decided to take the summer off. It would be a time to test the gradually emerging idea of a life lived out of the mainstream, a life of greater freedom and greater adventure, a life that would demand more from us and give more back. We were going to Guatemala, a country we'd already visited twice before and whose beauty had grabbed us in a visceral way. Was it true love or just a passing fancy? We figured we'd know by the summer's end.

It was love all right. Remembering it still causes a pain somewhere inside, like recalling a deeply felt but flawed love affair. But we knew that if we stayed and bought land, we'd be on the wrong side when the revolution came, no matter how enlightened our politics or our agriculture. So we came home. But not before we got a glimmer of a different kind of life—a life lived simply, shared with our children, and a life where those damnable walls between indoors and out, between man and nature, were not so impenetrable. We lived amidst waterfalls and orchids, volcanoes and a crater lake, but it is not these which I remember best. It is the sun-splashed, whitewashed room we shared, its furniture made out of slabs of wood supported by rocks, its casement windows flung open to hummingbirds and butterflies and to the sound of insects and wind and waterfall. I remember it because, as we slept and read and cooked and argued and groaned and laughed together there, we were a family.

When the summer was over we didn't come home and say, "Now we know what we want—how are we going to find it?" Only the young and unencumbered have the privilege of that single-mindedness. We did what everyone does after a very special vacation: we thought about it wistfully for a while, we wondered how we could make it last, and then we went about our business.

That winter Dick and I joined the almost one million other Americans reading *Mother Earth News* (more people than read *Business Week*, which is something to give one pause). Instead of bringing home Didion, Naipaul, and Kozinski from the library, Dick brought back *Five Acres and Security, Growing It*, and *Pasture Management*. On Sunday mornings, instead of vying for the Book Section, we began to race each other for the Real Estate Section of the *Chicago Sunday Tribune*. But while I loved to *talk* about moving to the country, I wasn't so sure I wanted to actually *do* it, for the fact is that my taste for adventure invariably runs smack against an equally powerful thrust for the conventional and continuity. This tends to make me an unreliable partner in any venture. "Yes!" I say, "Oh, yes!" to the vision, then tremble and pale and deny ever having said such a thing when confronted with the reality. And so it was now. With true perversity I spent the winter and spring bringing up the subject of moving to the country when it threatened to languish of neglect and shooting it down when it seemed to be getting serious.

Dick feels about the Mississippi River the way most of us feel about the ocean. The river, for him, is as awesome and romantic and worthy of contemplation as the idea that the next landfall is Spain for the fellow standing on the boardwalk in Atlantic City. I have no particular feeling for the river, but I like the countryside around it. It is a place of hills and fields and woods dotted here and there with silos and red barns, and of occasional sweeping views that are like suddenly finding yourself airborne. It is, in many ways, the Midwest's own Vermont. It is a curious fact about life here in the Midwest that those of us who live in Chicago have never colonized the surrounding territory to any appreciable extent. A New Yorker considers Long Island his backyard, Vermont the back forty and Connecticut, Massachusetts, New Hampshire, Maine, and the New Jersey shore provinces of the empire. Not so here. Chicagoans go to Door County, Wisconsin; New Buffalo, Michigan; and Mexico. Even Galena, an old river port and mining town blessed with extraordinary beauty and rich in history, seems perpetually on the brink of becoming a ghost town, although it has been described as "a crown jewel of American architecture." When summer came, it was to Galena that we turned.

When we'd called from the city to make an appointment with a local real estate agent, he'd dispensed with questions of time and place and had said, "Don't worry, I'll find you," and so he did, in the bar of the half-empty DeSoto House at five o'clock on a Friday night. Drawing a chair from the table next to our own, he sat astride it, pushed back his Stetson, and said, "Now what can I do for you folks?"

We told him we were interested in a farm—just looking, of course, but on the Galena River, if possible, since it would connect us with the Mississippi. As he continued to ask questions—how many acres? what would we raise? how much were we willing to spend? had we farmed before?—I began to feel distinctly uncomfortable. We were clearly indulging in a fantasy and wasting this nice man's time. But within the hour, we stood atop a hill, looking across a valley at the white spires and orange brick of Galena, now in miniature. In the opposite direction there was nothing, no human habitation, all the way to Iowa. There, he said, where the mist hung suspended over the distant, darkening trees—there's the Mississippi. Apple trees heavy with fruit led to a weathered gray farmhouse. A friendly dog wagged his tail and moaned when we petted him. If we were indulging in a fantasy, it had materialized before our very eyes.

"Yes! Oh, yes!" I whispered fiercely to Dick. The conservative, conventional side of me had yet to be heard from.

2

Finding

There was never any doubt that we would take it. There are certain things that you know, instantly, are right, that draw you to them as if they were speaking to you. A teacup, an old doll, an umbrella, a house—everyone has had the experience. If there had been any doubts, however, they would have been swept away by what we saw the following day. It was less a farm than a wilderness. Heavily wooded ridges dropped sharply to grassy valleys which gave way to narrower, more secret valleys which rose to higher hills and deeper woods. There were groves of giant oaks; rocky crags jutting from the earth riven by trees and abloom with ferns and lichens; startled hawks that screamed out of treetops and wheeled overhead. There were brambles of gooseberry, raspberry, and wild rose, and fields gone back to grasses taller than a man. And there was silence: a silence so deep that you could hear the sound of a hickory nut as it touched the ground. One could *own* this? It was inconceivable.

The house, on the other hand, was appalling, a house seemingly abandoned and yet so thickly personal that to cross the doorsill made one ill at ease. The farm was owned by two brothers in their sixties. Bob, the older, was married and lived in town with his wife Stella. Ed, a bachelor, had lived a reclusive life on the farm for thirty or forty years, gradually reducing his occupancy of the house to the periphery of its two wood stoves. Torn green shades, pulled to the windowsills, cut out most of the light that came through the grimy windows. The acrid smell of woodsmoke permeated the air and a fine dust of ash covered every surface. There was a tattered and stained velvet sofa, heaped with *Popular Mechanics* and *Prairie Farmer,* an iron bedstead, its bare mattress piled with quilts and newspapers, a table, a few chairs, a TV. Beyond this, every room, whatever its original purpose, was an attic. Stovepipes lay on beds. A saddle rode a sawhorse. A mirror reflected an outboard motor. Cartons full of empty Pringle potato-chip cans sat on trunks full of embroidered linens. Wallpaper flapped from walls, revealing on the crumbling plaster underneath the notation of some long-ago paperhanger: "April 18, 1917—cold day." Dead sparrows lay on the floor of one of the upstairs bedrooms, surrounded by their own droppings. Floors bulged in peculiar places and walls had watermarks in predictable ones. In the earthen cellar, ancient tires had been put down over the years like so many bottles of wine, and the brown and puckered husks of apples gone rotten some previous year sat in mute rows on a table rotting at a slower pace. Had the house been empty, we might have been able to envision what it might become. As it was, we could scarcely remember the pattern of its rooms after leaving. We knew it had no bathroom, no water, no heat except for that which came from the wood stoves, and no insulation, but we were buying a farm, not a house. We had hazy ideas about building our own; anything that would serve as shelter for a while was a dividend.

There was no price on the farm, the real estate agent told us. It wasn't even officially up for sale. We would have to make an offer. With the help of a friend who knew the value of farmland in this area, we came up with the figure of $850 an acre and phoned it from the city the next night. The offer was accepted. We had ourselves a farm. There was the matter of getting an easement for the mile-long lane that led to it, since it went through a neighbor's pasture, and a place would have to be found for Ed, but these were details.

After waiting a decent interval, we asked if we might visit again and bring the children. The trip was harrowing. We arrived in Galena at midnight and got the last room in the hotel, now swollen with tourists come to see the fall colors. The price, for a room with two double-beds and a crib, was fifteen dollars. After breakfast the next morning at a lunch counter where the coffee was still a dime a cup, we set out to launch the inflatable boat, a souvenir from our trip to Guatemala that we'd brought along so that we could see the property from the Galena River, which bounded it on two sides. The plan was to set out from a landing on the Mississippi, follow its banks to the Galena River, and go up the Galena River to the farm, beyond which lay the town. But the boys caught sight of a canoe rental as we drove through town, and anxious for them to have a good time on their first trip to the farm, we agreed to let them rent a canoe and to rendezvous with them on the river.

Some local fishermen looked us over as we inflated the boat and said, "It's pretty cold out there today." They were right. But the sky was that deep blue of autumn, the leaves overhead were a translucent yellow, and a kingfisher led the way. It took forty-five minutes to get to the rendezvous spot, and the boys, who had a much shorter distance to travel, weren't there. We continued upriver toward the town, and found them sitting in the canoe, drenched and dripping, their trembling visible from twenty yards. They had capsized the boat, they told us sheepishly, and Bill had lost his glasses, which I had purchased only the day before, to the bottom of the Galena River. We towed them into town and told them to find a warm place to wait for us since we had to go back to the landing on the Mississippi where we had left the car.

We ran out of gas three times. The first good samaritan exchanged his extra gas can for our empty one, which got us part way. The second had coldly and wordlessly given us a niggardly amount that got us within sight of the landing and the car. We paddled the rest of the way.

Bob had found out where we would be in the way that news travels in small towns, and had come to meet us, bringing Stella. We had never met, but she took my icy hands in her own and held them there all the way to the farm. It was a gesture of simple humanity, the kind of no-nonsense kindliness which we would experience again and again in our new environment.

After we'd all dried out and warmed up, we spent the rest of the day roaming the farm on foot, incredulous all over again that this much space and loveliness could belong to anyone. That it would soon belong to us was secondary. The revelation was that it was *there*—an acre for less than half of our annual tax bill in Evanston, a hundred acres for the price of a suburban townhouse.

As I watched the boys racing down hills, flinging frisbees across the pasture, and stumbling through woods, I felt the beginning of the conviction that we were doing something wonderful: something that was not just what we wanted, but that was *right*. As we left, Stella gave us a bag of watercress that would have made thirty bunches in the supermarket, and said, "Come back anytime."

We decided to treat ourselves to a celebratory dinner at a good restaurant before starting back, and chose the mansion on the hill we had seen on our way into town. I volunteered to scout the place while the rest waited in the car.

There was candlelight and white linen and a fire in the fireplace and French on the menu. I decided to bare my soul to the hostess. Look, I said, we weren't dressed properly because we'd spent the day on the river and our kids had fallen in and we had a toddler with us and we didn't have any cash, but we *needed* this and we had credit cards and would they take them and would they take us?

Of course, she said. You could wear anything anywhere in Galena and they didn't take credit cards but they would take our personal check. So we had steak and wine by candlelight in front of the fire, and the hostess watched over us and asked if everything was all right, and it was, it was. When we got into the car to go home, Kate asked me to sing to her, and as I progressed from the songs of the nursery to the "Battle Hymn of the Republic" (one of her favorites), Dick joined me and we sang a medley that reached across the years, across the eras of the nation's history, and—perhaps—across the space between the front seat and the back.

The boys didn't sing, but they didn't groan either.

Stella had said to come any time, and we did, almost every weekend as negotiations between our lawyers and the neighbor's lawyers over the easement for the road dragged on. But something peculiar was going on. There was no visible evidence of any preparation to move. We knew that the sale of the farm had taken the Brendels by surprise, that Bob hadn't been feeling well, and that readying it for our occupation would be infinitely more complex than any move we had ever undertaken. Besides the contents of the house where three generations had lived for over one hundred years, there were the contents of the barn, a grainery, and several sheds to be disposed of, scores of pieces of farm machinery, a herd of cattle, a flock of chickens, and a pair of horses. And then there was the question of where Ed would go. As the closing date drew near with a modicum of progress, it became increasingly awkward and increasingly worrisome. We didn't know what to do. It wasn't ours yet, and furthermore, the Brendels were becoming like a family to us. It was unthinkable to put any pressure on them, no matter how discrete. We did allow ourselves to gently probe when we could, but the responses were frustratingly oblique. A question about selling the livestock brought "We'll get around to it one of these days—don't you worry." An offer to help with the moving got "Oh, no, that's our job. We'll take care of it." And a discrete inquiry about plans for Ed got "Something will come along." So we waited, city impatience pinioned by country kindness. A bowl of hot soup when we checked in at Bob and Stella's on Friday night before going out to the farm. A bag of walnuts when we left. An offer to take care of Kate.

Meanwhile, we had plenty of time to consider what we wanted the farm to be, and to learn what it was. Our initial impression of its richness only deepened with familiarity. There were deer, beaver, skunk, and raccoon. There were bluebirds, tanagers, mourning doves, and eagles. Red-headed woodpeckers were as ubiquitous as robins in Evanston. But out of the two hundred acres, only sixty were tillable. An aerial map showed that the boundary lines formed more or less a rectangle, and within the rectangle the property was like a hand with fingers spread. The house, the barnyard, the orchard, and a hay field sat in the palm. The fingers were tillable fields, the space between them ravines, and the area between the hand and the rectangle, a series of interconnecting valleys that surrounded it all.

We could raise beef cattle on the rough land—it was standard practice in the area—but the capital required to start a herd was awesome. It would be fun we thought, allowing ourselves a flight of fancy, to raise some esoteric crop like ginseng or bittersweet, or to develop a herd of llamas or buffalo. In the meantime, we would feel our way, keeping our jobs.

Many of our choices of what we would do with the farm were dictated by an affinity for what Dick, a math major during college days, calls "the elegant solution." The Oxford English Dictionary defines elegance, when used in this manner, as "neatness, ingenious simplicity, convenience and effectiveness" and notes that "the etymological sense is choosing simply and carefully."

Sitting in our Evanston kitchen, we decided we would farm with horses because our tillable acreage was so small; because fuel is costly and scarce; and because horses return fertilizer to the soil. The sight of a hitched team pulling is also one of the most beautiful sights on earth.

We decided we would like to have the handsome, even elegant, composting toilet imported from Denmark, guaranteed to be odorless, because why use water, a precious resource, and install an expensive septic system when there was no need? We decided we would heat our house with wood and solar power, because we had an abundance of the former and a choice of sites that would enable us to take advantage of the latter. Why import oil from the Mideast and a furnace to use it from the city?

Along with the elegant solution, we were attracted by the idea of self-sufficiency. We had no desire to undertake the closed system in which you shear your own sheep, spin the wool, weave the cloth, and sew the clothes. But we liked relying on the farm for fuel, for

fresh vegetables, eggs, and meat, and for feed for whatever livestock we acquired.

If the above sounds breezy with confidence in what we
had done and were about to do, we were not. At least,
I was not. While Dick contemplated the new life with
unalloyed anticipation, I was assaulted by waves of un-
certainty. This was no mere change of locale, but a
plunge into the unknown: from a city/suburban exis-
tence to a rural America as strange as a foreign country;
from the comfort of family and friends to isolation; from
libraries, nursery schools, and ethnic restaurants to
. . . what? And why were we doing it? We were not
unhappy. We had, after all, a good life. It had taken us
a long time to reach this point. Moving was an earth-
quake and reconstruction took years.

These were Evanston thoughts. Sometimes weekends
on the farm banished them; other times they were inten-
sified. We would leave for the farm on a Friday night,
excited and happy, remembering the peak moments of
the weekend before and anxious to see what inroads Bob
and Ed had made on the mess, and arrive to find it virtually unchanged and utterly alien in its bleakness and
bone-chilling cold. It was a mortal blow. What in God's
name were we doing here? We weren't farmers. Nothing
in the world would make us farmers. It was all a monstrous mistake.

Then I would awaken to a sunrise so spectacularly
beautiful that there was nothing to do but jump out of
bed and race into the yard where I could watch it illumi-
nate the entire sky, a great upside-down bowl over our
hilltop. Or I would walk along the rocky ridge to the
farthest valley, the long narrow one I had claimed for my
own, and lie in the tall grass, utterly alone, watching two
hawks wheel over my head, and want never, ever to
leave.

There was never a magic moment when all doubts

were assuaged. They continued even after we had moved in. But gradually our old life became so pale and dull in comparison to the adventure that lay before us that I had, finally, no appetite for turning back.

3

Enduring

The day of possession came and went with as little ceremony as the due date for a library book. I think we went to a movie. It had become clear that titles, easements, and certified checks, matters of high solemnity in the city, were mere ephemera in the country. The real transaction that was taking place was the bequeathing of a farm held and worked by one family for more than a hundred years to city folks of good will, high spirits, and bottomless naïveté.

I treasure a letter from Stella that reads: "We are thrilled and awed by the ambition, courage, and speed of your expressed takeover. We say, 'Wonderful, great, and all that's good to you!' But with the winter fast approaching we feel we should caution you lest the hardships become too discouraging for the desired pleasures." We could never say we hadn't been warned.

The ambition that she referred to was our plan to move to the farm in February, after the first semester of school in Evanston had ended. Now that the farm was ours, we couldn't wait to begin our new life, even if we had to begin it in a house without heat or water in the middle of winter. Bob and Stella were plainly worried about our blithe attitude. They urged Kate and me to spend the night at their house in Galena when the temperature in the farmhouse on weekends began to plummet. They told us which wood made the hottest fire (hickory and red elm) and what to use for kindling (corn cobs soaked in kerosene). They said nothing when the flock of thirty or so chickens they had left us dwindled to a dozen because we hadn't locked them up at night. They watched with compassion our weekend attempts to cheer up the dismal farmhouse. By now, most of the contents of the house had been removed to the barn to be disposed of by an auction in the spring. Ed, however, was still there.

If Ed has a curiously passive role in this tale, it is because that is the way he is. He says little and shuns society. He lived alone on the farm for thirty or forty years with neither car nor telephone. The hunters who came each fall were his only visitors, except for Bob, who week after week, year after year, decade after decade, brought him his mail and his groceries. I think he enjoyed our weekend visits. We were a novelty, like the hunters. And we, for our part, enjoyed him. But we were also frustrated beyond words.

Each weekend we would arrive in high spirits and full of excitement, the car filled with brooms and buckets of paint, ready to clear the decks and clean the slate—and we would open the door to someone else's house. The refrigerator was filled with Ed's food; the ashtrays with Ed's cigarette butts; the rooms with Ed's possession. A man of average size, he began to fill the house like a genie, his presence suffocating us.

Hesitantly, we would broach the subject of a place for Ed with Bob and Stella. Once, we offered the idea of a house trailer on the property. Heaven knows there was enough room for all of us, and we were sensitive to the fact that the farm had been his entire world. "You know, it isn't a good idea to leave the house unoccupied during the week. You might come up and find your windows shot in," Bob would reply. We never knew whether the hazard was real or imagined. We didn't care. We wanted our farmhouse to be ours. At Thanksgiving, when Dick's and my families joined us on the farm, Ed moved into town with Bob and Stella. When we arrived the next weekend, he was back at the kitchen table, rolling a cigarette. In the end, nature intervened. A December blizzard dumped two feet of snow on the snaking, uphill, mile-long lane that led from the paved road to the farm. Bob brought out Ed in a snowmobile. By the time the road was passable again, we had made the house unmistakably ours.

If weekends with Ed were difficult, weekends without him were in some ways worse. Winter had set in with a vengeance. Whatever heat came from the two wood stoves just as quickly went. Not only was there no insulation, but the clapboard siding of the house was so split and cracked that a set of wind-chimes, placed in the living room in a forlorn attempt at decoration chimed all weekend long, all winter long, and crystals of ice lined the living-room wall. The children slept in sleeping bags, and emerged in the morning with their noses and cheeks red with cold. In our own bedroom, the glass of water on the night table had a layer of ice by dawn. The worst part was getting up in the morning, the normal need to relieve oneself aggravated to desperate urgency by the cold, but unable to do anything about it until we had donned jeans, sweaters, boots, down jackets, and mittens for the trip to the outhouse.

One Monday morning when we had returned to Evanston from the weekend's discomfort, I went out and bought half a dozen thermometers from the local hardware store. The next weekend I put one in every room.

They ranged from seventy in the kitchen when the wood stove was roaring to eighteen degrees in the outlying rooms.

Despite the hardships, we looked forward to the Christmas vacation period when we could spend an entire two weeks on the farm. Once there, we had no choice. An ice storm coated the long ascending drive. We were stranded, without telephone, in two feet of snow coated by ice so thick and slick that we ended up sprawling every time we walked out to get wood. My mother was due to arrive on the Blackhawk from Chicago at 9:30 on Christmas Eve. Without a telephone, there was no way to tell her to stay where she was, so at eight o'clock on Christmas Eve, we awakened Kate, bundled her warm and drowsy body in snowsuit and quilts, and went out into the cold night. All evening I had scraped away the ice on the inside of the kitchen window with a spatula to read the thermometer outside. Ten below. Thirteen below. Fifteen below. Nineteen below. It was the kind of cold that draws the nostrils together, and dries the mucous membrane at the back of the throat, making it difficult to speak. There was only one way to go: cross-country. We drove through the apple orchard to the pasture, across the pasture to the fence that separated it from the neighbor's cornfield. Working with bare hands —gloves were too clumsy—Dick cut the wires of the fence in the light from the car's headlights. We drove through the cornfield to another fence, another field, hoping we'd be forgiven our trespass by a neighbor not yet met. Finally we gained access to his barnyard, and slid out onto the road.

The town, beautiful in all seasons, was a fairytale. To the gingerbread of the architecture, now frosted in snow, was added a tree in every window, a wreath on every door, and often boughs of pine or huge candy-canes tied to gates and fences. Lanterns out of Dickens shed a golden light over a silent, empty Main Street. Mr. Pettigout, officially the station-master but in heart a shepherd to all travelers, greeted us warmly and welcomed us to the plain confines of the clean and tidy station as if it were an inn.

As the train came into view, sounding its plaintive whistle, I remembered the Christmas trips by train my mother and I had made to my grandparents' farm when I was a little girl: the people sitting on suitcases in the aisle or on the arms of seats or swaying overhead, the easy camaraderie, the sharing of magazines and Christmas cookies and family histories between strangers, and then the arrival of the red-cheeked conductor into the warm car, the cold clinging to his very clothes, abruptly severing the connections that had been formed. "Cassopolis! . . . Next stop Cassopolis!"

As we drove home I asked her if it had been like that. No, she said, there had been only a few people on the train, and no one had spoken. Perhaps that is one of the reasons we have chosen to live in Galena.

We have had prettier Christmases, but I think none will ever equal that one. The spindly cedar we cut ourselves with an axe and stuck in a pail in a corner, its only decorations Kate's stuffed animals stuck in its branches, was a sorry sight compared to the magnificent trees that had stretched from the foyer to the second floor landing in our Evanston home, heavy with treasured ornaments, ablaze with twelve strings of old-fashioned lights, but no fire had ever been as warm as that which greeted our return, nor any gift as welcome as the red union suit from my mother that I opened on Christmas morning.

If the bathroom situation, for which the red union suit was my armor, was bad, it was not as bad as the kitchen.

All those instinctive gestures of ordinary living—rinsing out a glass, tossing peelings into the garbage, reaching for canned goods—were stymied. All food with any liquid in it—a can of beans for example—had to be stored in the refrigerator since, paradoxically, that was the only place it wouldn't freeze and burst during our absence. Trash had to be separated according to what could be burned and what could not, and the unburnable hauled back to Evanston so it wouldn't attract rats or mice.

We hauled water from the barnyard in five-gallon collapsible jugs of the sort used by campers. Its color, pale orange, was alarming, but it apparently hadn't hurt Ed. We set the jug on the counter horizontally, so that its spigot hung over the edge and set a pail under it to catch the drips and to use as a slop jar. If the expression is ugly, the reality was uglier still: a witches' brew of milk from the bottom of cereal bowls, uneaten soup, orange juice, leftover beer, and hot chocolate. I recently watched an interview with a couple who were living a pioneer life in a Williamsburg-type recreation. What, they were asked, was the modern convenience they missed most? A drain, they responded without hesitation. I would agree. We heated water for doing the dishes in a kettle on the wood stove, and did them in dish pans set on the counter. There was no way we could bathe, so we didn't, for days at a time. The inconveniences could be laughed at, because they came and went with the hour of the day. The cold, however, was always there.

You don't have to move to Alaska to freeze to death, as the stories of the elderly dying in urban apartments where the heat has been turned off abundantly prove. All you need is very cold weather, no heat, and the inability to get help. There was a moment when it seemed like it might happen to us. I guess I knew it wouldn't come to that, but the experience left us with a much greater respect for both weather and wood.

The deep snow that had made it so difficult to get out on Christmas Eve had made it equally difficult to get into the woods to replenish our firewood supply. Nevertheless, we had to try, for when Dick returned to the farm from a few days in the city at the end of our Christmas vacation period, we were down to our last log. Not only was there no wood, but the needle on the gas gauge of the four-wheel drive, which would get us to where the wood was, was on empty.

We drove into town to get gas, and while there, stopped to wish Stella and Bob and Ed a Happy New Year, staying longer than we'd planned. On our way back up the hill to the house, our wheels started spinning so we backed down to try it again. On the second attempt, while trying to avoid the icy patch our tires had made, Dick steered the car to the outermost edge of the road. Only it wasn't. There was a sickening sensation of falling, and then a grab. We were hanging over a steep embankment. We crawled out and, seeing there was nothing to be done, began trudging up the hill through the thigh-high snow carrying Kate. When we got to the house, the stove was cold, the sun had set and the temperature was twelve degrees and falling. Dick set off with the chain saw and the toboggan for a plum tree and I sat by the CB radio he'd brought back from the city for such an emergency saying, "Breaker, breaker, do you read me?" into the night. The night did not respond.

By the time Dick returned, exhausted and numb with cold, the temperature outside was ten below, and in the house, thirty above. While he monitored the radio, I made a fire and hoped that the wood he'd cut would last the night. Long after I had given up hope of a response, we were startled by a crackle and a buzz followed by a cheerful voice that said, "We read you loud and clear.

What's the trouble?" The feeling was exactly like birth: relief, excitement, and laughter followed by tears. It was the sheriff's office and they said that they would get a tow truck in or us out the next morning. They also said they would call the Brendels for us and ask them to call the Dubuque airport where the boys were expected the next day, and have someone tell them to fend for themselves until we could get there.

About an hour after the conversation, as we sat in front of the stove warming ourselves, we heard a noise at the door. Bob Brendel walked in, his face white with cold. After getting the call from the sheriff's office, he had driven to a neighbor's house, parked his car there, and walked the mile across the fields from that house to our own through the deep snow and the ten-below cold and the cutting wind in order to see for himself that we were all right. After all, he said, what are friends for?

The plum tree Dick cut that night was the last wood we would have that winter. Snowfall after snowfall made it impossible to get into the woods. But the hardships, far from being the discouragement that Stella had feared, only made us more determined. We brought coal in duffel bags and garbage cans from an Evanston building whose owner wanted to get rid of it, and when that source dried up, we stopped each weekend at a coalyard in a tiny town en route and filled the back compartment of the Toyota with it, shovelful by shovelful.

If those weeks were a test of our ability and will to survive in our new environment, they were also an introduction to the joys of it. In the city, I had rejoiced to thick-falling snowflakes, to the creaking of ice-encased branches, and to the high drama of solemn weather reports on the nightly news. But I never *did* anything. We who live in the so-called temperate climates are like children brought to the YMCA pool to learn to swim. Something deep inside responds, but we just can't get the hang of it before the time is up. And besides, there's all that business of changing clothes. It's fitting that the term "cabin fever" has been appropriated by city-dwellers, for they are the ones who suffer from it most.

On the farm, I could barely bring myself to come inside. True, the house was not all that welcoming. True, a snowy countryside is more inviting than a slushy city. But I think it has to do more with a kind of equilibrium between indoors and out. We would wear the same long underwear, the same jeans, the same wool socks and down vests from Friday night to Sunday night so that going out was a matter of supplementation rather than transformation. And when we came in, there were no highly polished floors or fancy carpets to worry about. The storm door banged as often as a screen door does in the summertime. Out to get wood. Out to get water. Out to the outhouse. Out just to *be* out.

We cross-country skied with the grace of giraffes and the joy of children except for Kate, who preferred to roll over on her back, waggle her skis at the sky, and giggle. We lay down in the snow and made angels with our arms.

We sledded down the hill we couldn't drive up and we followed animal tracks with fascination. The sun and the cold and the snow were intoxicating. We couldn't get enough. But the isolation, so dramatic and exciting on a winter's night with the snow and temperature falling, continued to nag at me. What would it be like when we actually lived here?

4

Ours

I suppose that if I had stopped to think about it, I might have realized that the town we saw across the snow-covered valley was a town with people in it who would someday become friends, and a town that would someday become home in a way that a house alone can never be. But we were so isolated by the weather, our location, and the primitive quality of the life we were leading that I felt as removed from Galena as from Chicago itself.

One Sunday afternoon as we gathered our things together for the trip back to the city, we thought we heard a car, but immediately discounted it and went back to bagging garbage. The knock on the door, however, was unmistakable.

"We saw the smoke from your chimney . . . hope you don't mind . . . sorry to intrude . . . "—the words tumbled from a small woman with sleek blond hair and good bones, accompanied by an equally attractive man with smiling blue eyes. A flurry of activity followed: shaking off of winter gear, chairs pulled from other rooms, debris of lunch swept away, coffee offered.

Their names were Bea and Michael Limback and they lived just down the road. They had tried to welcome us several times before, but each time had had to turn back because of the road. They, too, had moved from the Chicago area. Yes, they lived here the year around. The schools? They were okay. They had two daughters the same ages as our sons, and they had adjusted beautifully. But what was really wonderful was that in a school so small everybody participated in everything. We would love it, they promised. Wait until spring!

We took them through the house. Only humor would help, so we laughed and traded early horror stories, the dead sparrows in our house, the bats in theirs. They thought it beautiful and us brave and I loved them both. But never once did I believe that their house could ever have been anything like ours.

They asked us to dinner the following weekend and all week long I looked forward to it. I was sure their farmhouse would turn out to be a Trianon, a bit of Lake Forest amusingly placed on the banks of the Mississippi. I would be disappointed, but I would like them anyway. Instead, we found a plain old farmhouse, as plain within as without, and almost as cold as our own. Spare to the point of severity, the few treasures—a silver candelabra, a magnificent mahogany table—reminded me of the pianos lashed to the back of wagon trains one hundred fifty years before. It was clear that in what they had left behind, as well as in what they had taken, they had made a statement about the life they would lead.

We saw them frequently, using their bathroom for showers ("Everyone in Galena has had to bathe in someone else's house at one time or another," said Bea), but it wasn't until much later that I asked her to tell me the story of their move.

They had lived the typical Lake Forest life, she said, which is to say the life lived in all enclaves of the well to do: the socially secure family, the comfortable home, the private education, the friends with names like Missie and Muffie and the young men whose names ended in Roman numerals.

"I'd always assumed that when I married I'd live just like my parents and friends, and when Mike and I married, we did at first. The gatehouse . . . the flower garden . . . the good works. It was all very swish—the Bath and Tennis Club, the seats on boards, the benefits.

"Mike was in business with his father—adhesives— and it was getting more and more profitable, so they decided to invest in real estate—a farm in Galena. I signed the contract, but for months I didn't even see it. My attitude was 'that's fine—it has nothing to do with me.' It was just an investment. And when I did see it I thought it was hokey and icky. All that nineteenth-century farm equipment and the kitchen looked like an Easter egg—pink walls, turquoise cabinets, yellow insides. But Mike loved it from the first and so I came out because it was the thing to do, to be with him. Then spring came and I planted a garden. I guess that was the beginning. And we started bringing favorite things, books and vases and stuff like that. But it was still just something to talk about at cocktail parties back home. People would say, 'Oh, you brave souls!', and I would feel smug.

"Sometimes we would go for walks and look at each other and say, 'Is this really ours?', but other times it would rain or the pipes would freeze and I'd hate it and I'd hate Mike. I usually spent the entire weekend in the house cleaning and yelling at everyone and then I thought, 'Why am I doing this? I really *like* these kids,' so I made a decision to let go, and get outside and have fun. But the business of coming back on Sunday nights was awful. The traveling back and forth was exhausting in itself, and I'd have to shift gears so dramatically after the weekend. Gradually, I began to compare myself to the people who were my friends. I saw a lot of grasping, a lot of frightened people, and I didn't feel like one of them. They were fighting for something that just didn't matter. It was just going from flower to flower . . . parties . . . drinking. There wasn't enough time to get into anything or to have real relationships.

"Then Mike's father died and the farm became ours. Suddenly, I found myself wanting to come out here alone, or with just one of the children. I remember once it took us eight hours to get here because little Mike and I stopped at all the places Mike would never stop for. We had all kinds of adventures. We took walks together and we'd sleep together so we wouldn't be afraid. And farmers would stop by to see how we were doing.

"For five years we talked about moving here full time, and when Mike was able to sell out part of the business and still have an income, we did. It was two years ago last August and I'll never forget putting my clothes in the closet and the food in the refrigerator and thinking, 'When Sunday night comes, *I won't have to go back.*'

"My life is mine now. It's not an appendage of my parents. It's my mark on the world. *I chose it.* And living here has made me realize I'm tough inside. I can cope. I can do things I never in a million years dreamed I could do, and I know things I don't even know I know. I'm not afraid any longer. Life is simple now. It seems like it ought always to have been."

Bea was an unlikely pioneer, but so, in fact, were many of the women who moved west a century before. Pioneers, I would learn, are still with us and come from all walks of life, for different reasons and with different goals. The Limbacks were not the least likely.

One of our reasons for choosing Galena was that we hoped we would find, behind the tasteful storefronts that bespoke an urban sensibility, some compatible souls. I did not think I could survive in a pure farming community—a cluster of houses around a grain elevator, a grocery store, and a post office—nor did I think the kids could make such a transition. But neither did I want to live in an expatriate enclave. And so, while I took pleasure in the graceful antique shops on Main Street, and in the beautiful old homes on the bluff that rises sharply from it, I took equal comfort in the dusty shop windows with forlorn "For Rent" signs, the pickup trucks parked diagonally to the curb, and the sight of couples in matched bowling jackets advertising "Dutch and Kate's" or "Race's Paradise Bar." It seemed a town solidly based in the prosaic, if not, in some instances, in the downright dowdy. Down at the heels, topped by white spats.

During the worst of the winter, our contact with it had been limited to a quick stop at the Okey Dokey upon arrival late Friday night for milk and bread and the *Galena Gazette,* and sometimes a Saturday night dinner at the Log Cabin. We traveled en masse: a trip to town with its promise of warmth and an indoor toilet was an event no one wanted to miss, and there was always the possibility of not making it back up the hill. But though the distance between our own front door and the tall, steel floodgates that are the town's was only three miles, our descents from our hilltop were as surely the visits of tourists as if we had come from the city for a day of sightseeing: the self-congratulation; the feeling of adventure; the impressions instantly framed and shared like Polaroid prints. The presence of others, especially those near and dear, is a kind of insulation; and so I got to know the town alone, with a basket of dirty laundry and a shopping list.

It was a late winter afternoon, dark enough for cars to have their headlights on, cold enough for the rain to turn to sleet, and the sleet to a thin sheet of ice. I went from launderette to bank, bank to drugstore, drugstore to supermarket, taking deep pleasure in familiarity; in repeating here the homely tasks I'd performed a million times before in a dozen other environments. But there were totally unexpected grace notes here, not one or two as sometimes happens in the city, but as a continuous counterpoint to commerce. Clerks came from behind counters in stores clearly designed for self-service and said, "Can I help you?" Cashiers asked about the weather outside and said, "Drive carefully." Baggers carried groceries to cars, and I watched, astonished, as a second checkout line was opened because the first had *three people* waiting in it. If the shopkeepers were friendly and courteous, so were the shoppers. I saw people stand quietly and patiently in the supermarket aisle, waiting until someone blocking it in a trance of indecision moved on, foregoing even the discrete cough or polite "excuse me" that would have made their presence known.

After my chores were done, I decided to treat myself to a luxury, to have my hair, thick with the plaster dust of a demolition project at the farm, shampooed. I walked into the Armageddon Beauty Shop at five minutes before six. The proprietor was alone with her last customer. I apologized for my spontaneous appearance, and asked if she could she take me. She looked at the clock, debated with herself, then smiled and said, "Why not?" When I was ready to leave, I asked her how much I owed her. "Nothing," she said. "Consider it a welcome to Galena."

Getting to know the Limbacks on the one hand, and the town on the other, made all the difference in my own attitude toward the life I would soon take up in earnest. I had a friend. Galena was no longer a stage-set and I was no longer a spectator. I could hardly wait for the school-year to end and my new life to begin. But with the waning of winter there were other problems to be faced. By sheer virtue of living in Ed's house all those weekends, it had become ours, for better or worse. What were we going to do with it?

Dick and I have never worked particularly well together. He operates by the seat of his pants, whereas I am in love with planning and the planner's tools—lists, priorities, timetables, schedules, etc. We also have diametrically opposing views on the merits of self-reliance. I figure if God wanted us to build our own house, or to rebuild Ed's, he would have made us architects. Dick abhors the cult of the expert. Clearly we were not the kind of people who should undertake a massive do-it-yourself renovation together.

One of the results of our difference in style was that I felt abandoned and bitter when he proceeded in the way that was natural to him—getting up in the morning, for example, and taking a crowbar to the side of the house to see what lay underneath; but I lacked the confidence and skills—and the desire—to join him. I was a writer, damn it! Not a carpenter or an electrician! I didn't know how to do what I wanted done, and, thank you, I didn't care to learn. I just wanted it *done.* I wanted to start *living* in my new world.

Easter came early that year, and we spent the week preceding it on the farm. It was a week of high winds, freezing rains, and low temperatures that was especially disheartening after a winter such as we had just been through. On Good Friday morning, as I stood at the sinkless counter filled with gelid dishes in that cold kitchen with the walls coming down around me and the rain pouring down outside I realized I couldn't go on and said so. It wasn't a challenge or a solicitation of sympathy—just the truth. I don't know what I expected

Dick to say or do—when you are miserable you are beyond thinking about such things—but what he did was to put his arms around me and what he said was, "Look, perhaps we'll have to build a house from scratch. Perhaps we'll even have to get a place in the city and commute back and forth. *But we will survive.*"

Spring came finally, and for each ravaging of the spirit that was occurring within the house was a restorative to be had merely by stepping outside. For each estrangement over what to do and how to do it, there was the rediscovery of all that we both loved, and renewed love for each other *because* of the love of those things. The man who took a crowbar to the wall now gently lifted a log in the woods to see if there were any salamanders underneath, painted my hand with bloodroot, and called to me again and again, "Nance! Come here! You've got to see this!" Together, we explored the river, rocks, woods, and fields. And *exulted*. So *this* was spring! I'd always considered it a conceit of poets, a pale and poor watercolor of a season compared to the bold calligraphy of winter. Miserly. Withholding. But this was generous. A great, rippling expansion, gathering momentum, swelling.

I remember the first wildflower, its stem as small and fragile as a blade of grass, and on the stem what looked like twenty tiny butterflies of palest pink, each a carving.

I remember discovering the first *mass* of green, the bright, clear, radiant green of hundreds of young ferns, growing on a hidden, south-facing slope down by the river where all else was still brown and rotting.

I remember the gray, pitted, volcanic-looking rocks suddenly abloom with tender columbine, soft mosses, and brilliant lichens in silver, yellow, and orange.

I remember gathering nettles—our first proud foraging—plunging them into cold water to remove the sting, and cooking them for dinner.

I remember Kate saying, "Is it time to take our clothes off yet?" and Dick bathing in the horse trough.

As the season progressed, our weekends stretched to three days, then four, until finally we would take turns spending alternate weeks at the farm. There was too much to do to afford the luxury of both being in the same place, and what was happening on the farm was too wonderful to go unwatched. The hens had begun to lay eggs; the carp and buffalo fish were spawning in the pond; the cherry and apple trees were in blossom; the nasturiums and peas were already being overtaken by weeds, and the men were arriving—O happy day!—to lay the pipes that would bring water from the barnyard to the house.

Meanwhile, back in Evanston, we spent our days performing the dreary chores necessary to ready a house for sale: cleaning, plastering, painting, packing—dreary not because we felt sadness at our impending departure, but because this house was now as dead to us as the crumbled roses of a long-ago corsage I found at the bottom of a box of memorabilia.

As I moved back and forth between the two towns, Evanston and Galena, I became increasingly aware of the differences between them. I would emerge from the Evanston supermarket enraged as always at the twenty-minute wait at the checkout counter, at the cashier who still didn't recognize me after four years and god knows how many thousands of dollars worth of groceries, at the ridiculous "Reduced" rack with its mushy bananas and blackened tomatoes, a lordly nickel knocked off their price in deference to their inedibility . . . and then I would think of Galena, where the checkout woman already called me Nancy and always asked how things were going on the farm, where the stock boy would leave what he was doing and walk with me down the aisles to show me where the olives were, and where Mr. Stair, the owner, bags and carries groceries alongside of the high school boys he hires for the job. I would sit wearily in some left-turn lane in Skokie, miles of heavy traffic from home, wanting only to be finished with this insane rushing around by car—and think of the clean, finite profile of Galena, as simple as a primitive, visible in entirety at a single glance. I would crawl wearily into bed at night, only to remember I had parked on the "wrong" side of the street . . . and think longingly of our silent, starry, hilltop.

I felt boxed-in by buildings and overwhelmed by commerce, estranged from the natural world that had come to seem, increasingly, the "real" world. If there were marked differences between the two towns, I was also discovering that I was a different person in each. In an environment that was frequently rushed, rude, and indifferent, I, also, was often rushed, rude, and indifferent. In a relaxed and courteous environment, I, too, became relaxed and courteous.

With the arrival of warm weather, Bob and Ed were almost daily visitors to the farm, slowly emptying the barn, grainery, and sheds of a thousand artifacts of farming for the auction that soon would be held to dispose of them. Nothing is ever thrown away on a farm. Three-legged chairs, bottomless bushel baskets, rusted-out horse troughs, buckets without handles, treadless tires, bits of tin and pieces of glass, bottles and boxes, old salves and chemicals—all have their uses and all eventually end up on the auction wagon.

If I had been eager to clear our Evanston house of our own possessions, I could hardly wait to see the farm emptied of Bob's and Ed's, but as the day of the auction approached, I found myself resentful at the thought of scores of pickups gouging our road, still boggy with spring rains. I didn't want strangers tramping through my orchard, poking into my barn, looking at my view! And I certainly didn't care for turning my kitchen into a cashier's office! As I got crosser and crosser, I realized that what I was feeling was the territorial imperative, as old as the earth, as new as the most recently arrived red-winged blackbird broadcasting his claim from the telephone wire. The farm was mine.

The day of the auction dawned bright and beautiful. Stella was the first to arrive, with baskets of ham and potato salad, coleslaw and cake, followed by the auction personnel with their cashboxes and card tables. Soon the hilltop was swarming with people. As Stella introduced us to everyone she knew, I felt proud and shy, happy and nervous, and all in all, greatly like a bride. We basked in the good wishes and responded to the curiosity as best we could. Yes, we were going to farm it. No, we hadn't decided yet if we would rent any of it out. Yes, it was true that we intended to use horses. No, we'd never farmed before. Yes, it *was* a beautiful day, and we were very glad and grateful to be here.

And we were. The changing of the guard had been long and difficult. Perhaps that's the way it should be. At any rate we were, at last, citizens of West Galena Township, Jo Daviess County, state of Illinois. It was good to be home.

PART TWO

5

Of Lead and the River

"Towns were never intended as objects of worship . . . but if it were possible to have such gods . . . we should choose one with a marked character of appearance; of hills and valleys, of beetling cliffs and quiet dells, far rather than a city of tame curvature or a level plain."

Galena Daily Advertiser, 1856

Even to its natives, the Midwest is dull.

We will, of course, take exception if someone from another part of the country calls it to our attention, but among ourselves we know it to be true. Some of us have been known to move our homes one hundred miles from our places of work for the privilege of living where there is a visible gradient; to drive two hundred miles of a Sunday to picnic on a sand dune. Others pretend that flatness is a virtue, pointing out that they can see for miles, but neglecting to say what it is that they can see.

Of all the midwestern states, it is Illinois that suffers the most from the indifferent hand of nature. Indiana has its covered bridges and Utopian colonies, Wisconsin its North Woods and Indian names, and Iowa its groaning board. Michigan has sand dunes and Minnesota has

lakes. Kansas has Dorothy. Illinois has Chicago, soy-
beans, and corn, and after that there is little to say.

Even the Cinderella of the Midwest has had her moments, however, and as a result, there exists secreted
away in its northwest corner a small kingdom as sternly
beautiful as Vermont, as rich in history as the Hudson
River valley, and as romantic as New Orleans.

Its name is Jo Daviess County.

In cartographers' renderings of the world as it was a
million years ago during the Ice Age, which show a
North American continent covered by glaciers from the
Arctic Circle to the Ohio and Missouri rivers on the
south, there is a small shaded area about two dozen counties large along the Mississippi where Wisconsin and
Illinois meet. This is the famous "driftless" area which
survived on four separate occasions the leveling force of
the massive movements of ice in much the same manner
as a rock that divides a stream. Had the depth of the
stream been greater, or the rock been smaller, it would
have been submerged under "drift," the geologists' word
for the earth, sand, gravel, and boulders deposited by the
glaciers. As it happened, the rock (in this case, the Wisconsin highlands to the north) diverted the glaciers and
there survives in this generally flat and unremarkable
part of the world a record of an earlier and wilder
beauty.

A topographic map of the area as it is today looks like
nothing so much as a scattering of oak leaves after a
windstorm: their lobes, its hills; the spaces etched by the
lobes, its valleys. It is what farmers call "rough ground,"
meaning so hilly and rocky that by and large it is good
for little but grazing cattle. Its steep hillsides and ravines
are filled with timber and brush and the wild creatures
which seek such cover; its slopes and bottoms are pat-
terned with the fields of corn and hay grown for winter

forage. Across the horizon line march mounds whose protective crust of churt was laid down during the Silurian Age, 320 million years ago. Waters run off the hills and out of springs to carve creek-beds where watercress grows like a swaying carpet, and to fill rivers that empty into the Mississippi. Beauty, however, is not all that the glaciers left undisturbed. They also left one of the richest deposits of lead ore in North America lying close to the surface, awaiting man's discovery.

The French were first.

From the mid-1600s onward, the French explorers returned from the Upper Mississippi Valley with tales of mineral wealth, and in 1699 Le Sueur and Iberville set out from New Orleans with a troop of thirty men to study the region. On 25 August 1700 Le Sueur recorded in his journal that there was, on the east bank of the great river, a small river "that comes from the north at the mouth and flows from the northeast" where "seven leagues to the right there is a lead mine a league and a half inland." The discovery of "La Riviere de la Mines" was duly noted by William de Lisle, geographer for the French Academy of Sciences, on a map published in Paris in 1703, but it would be another hundred years before "La Riviere" would be exploited for its lead (*galena* in Latin) or the frontier town which took its name from the mineral would spring up on its banks.

Early in the month of April in 1823, a band of forty-three men, women and children assembled on the levee in Cincinnati. Led by Moses Meeker, an enterprising lead prospector, they were there to board the keelboat *Col. Bumford,* headed for "La Riviere de la Mines" (now called the Fever River) eleven hundred miles distant. During the preceding winter, they had purchased mining equipment and provisions sufficient to last them for a year in the wilderness: seventy-five tons of freight in all. At the captain's signal, the keelboat glided slowly down the Ohio. The party gained the Mississippi after thirty days, and began the struggle upstream against its current. After eighty miles of pushing by pole and pulling by means of brush along the river's banks, the *Col. Bumford* saw the steamship *Virginia,* which had just surmounted the treacherous Rock River Rapids to the south, becoming the first steamboat ever to ascend the Upper Mississippi. Meeker asked John Crawford, the *Virginia*'s captain, if he would pull the heavily laden keelboat, but Crawford refused on the grounds that the swift current often brought his own craft to a halt. By the time the keelboat arrived at the Fever River settlement, the *Virginia* had completed the trip to Fort Snelling, three hundred miles to the north, returned to Saint Louis, four hundred miles to the south, reloaded and passed the *Col. Bumford* again on its way to Fort Snelling a second time. It had taken the Meeker party thirty-one days to travel four hundred miles.

What they found upon gaining the Fever were a few rude log cabins six miles from its mouth, a few crude smelting furnaces, and two thousand Indians dotting the hillsides and ravines. Meeker and his party set to work, spending the first year "mostly building furnaces, houses, stables, and in digging a well." Meeker wrote, "In the month of August I had the census taken; there were seventy-four persons—men, women and children, white and black." Forty-three of them had arrived with Meeker.

Soon after Meeker's arrival, miners began filtering in from Kentucky and Missouri. Some came overland in covered wagons drawn by mule and oxen; others came up the river in keelboats. Travel was difficult by either land or water. Those traveling overland faced four hundred miles of prairie with neither road nor settlement after leaving Vandalia to the south. Those traveling by river faced a journey so arduous that a contemporary reader of their chronicles cannot help but be moved by their determination. The keelboats that they used were long, low, flat-bottomed boats, fifty to sixty feet in length and ten feet abeam, and were pushed by poles or pulled by men or mules when towpaths were accessible. But if the banks were steep or tangled, or the water was high as it often was in the spring when such migrations usually took place, they proceeded by bushwacking or cordelling. Bushwacking was leaning out over the edge of the craft and grasping anything that presented itself— bush, tree, grass—and inching the boat along the banks by that means. Cordelling was attaching a long rope to the bow of the boat, throwing it about a tree some distance ahead, and then pulling up, hand over hand, until the tree was reached, and beginning all over again. Not infrequently, a keelboat's passengers could still see at nightfall the morning's starting point.

Since many of the miners came north in the spring, and returned to the south in the fall before cold weather struck and the river froze, they were called "suckers" after the fish of the same habit. Those who came up from Missouri were called "pukes" because, it was said, Missouri had taken an emetic and spewed all its miners north to Galena. Finally, there were the "badgers," the ones who dug in, living in huts or caves in the rock for the winter.

Shortly after the Meeker party's arrival, the Federal government began to pay serious attention to the area, appointing Army Lieutenant Martin Thomas of Saint Louis "Superintendent of the Lead Mines of the Upper Mississippi." Approximately one hundred fifty thousand acres of the mineral land had been reserved by the U.S.

government by treaty with the Indians in 1816 and Thomas was to be its lord and master. It was to Thomas that a miner went for a permit to work a tract of the public domain in exchange for a rent of 10 percent of all lead discovered, for permission to build a cabin, to cultivate a garden and to cut down a tree. He could not sell his lead except to a licensed smelter; neither could he own a lot on which to build a house. It was reclaimable by the government on thirty days' notice, a practice which continued for another decade.

Nevertheless, with the breakup of the ice in the spring of 1827, America's first mining boom was on. Adventurers poured into Saint Louis and the levee was thronged with impatient men awaiting transportation up the Mississippi to the Fever River. By the close of navigation that season, thirteen steamboats had made their way upriver to the boom town, and had brought out five million pounds of lead. In the following year, ninety-nine steamboats had made the journey and had brought out eleven million pounds.

The rough settlement on the banks of the Fever had become "such a place as no one could conceive of without seeing it," wrote Dr. Horatio Newhall, an early settler, to his brother in Massachusetts. "Strangers hate it and residents like it. The appearance of the country would convince anyone it must be healthy, yet, last season, it was more sickly than Havana or New Orleans. There is no civil law here, nor has the Gospel yet been introduced. . . . The public smelters, of which I am one . . . are the great men of the country. . . . [Last year] there were four log buildings in Galena. Now there are one hundred and fifteen houses and stores in the place. It is the place of deposit for lead and provisions for all the mining country. There is no spot in America of the same size where there is one-fourth of the capital, or where so much business is done. . . . There are comparatively few females. Hence, every female, unmarried, who lands on these shores, is immediately married [including] little girls fourteen and even thirteen years old." Shortly after Newhall's letter, the Gospel arrived in the person of the Reverend Aratus Kent, a Yale graduate who had asked the American Home Missionary Society for "a place so hard that no one else would take it." "We are thrown together like the tenants of the graveyard without any order," the Reverend wrote to a friend back east. "There are people of every country and character, and you may see in one day Indians, French, Irish, English, German, Swiss and Americans in such a variety of national customs and costumes as are rarely to be met with in any other place."

Only five years after the Meeker party's arrival, Galena had become the foremost town north of Saint Louis and east of Detroit, with a school, a post office, a preacher, a newspaper, "forty-two stores and warehouses, twenty-two porter cellars and groceries, and a goodly number of lawyers and physicians." Though it was still a rude frontier town, there were ten or twelve balls within a brief period, and according to Dr. Newhall they were "managed with a degree of propriety and decorum scarcely to be expected in this wild country. I should have imagined myself in some eastern city rather than in the wilds of the Upper Mississippi [where] only 12 miles off is a large Fox village where I have witnessed the Indian dance around a fresh-taken scalp." While the good doctor was undoubtedly enjoying himself at the expense of his friends back east, there would, in fact, be Indian troubles before long.

Many of the settlers, like Newhall and Kent, had come from the east and looked to it for their standards of propriety, but others in the little town took pride in its frontier spirit and ways. "A lady here will travel 45 miles to a ball," a young gentleman reported, "and not be as much fatigued as one in Pittsburgh who only walked two squares." Nor was the east the only frame of reference. As the Reverend Kent had noted, Galena was already becoming a cosmopolitan place where the northerner and southerner, Irish and German, French and Welsh, mingled and created a far more open society than that of towns with a more gradual growth and a more homogenous population. "The stores are open on the Sabbath," a traveler wrote, "and the beer halls are crowded with light-spirited customers and from many a half-opened window we even hear the whining tones of a violin played by an unpracticed hand." Another commented more tersely: "Much vice and dissipation going on."

While the residents of the town were comporting themselves at balls and beer halls, the miners out in the diggings were becoming increasingly restive under the government's restrictions. Many miners had passed far beyond the government's boundaries into Indian territory. Some were squatters; others had paid the Indians for the privilege. Why, they began to ask, if the land belongs to the Indians, should we pay rent to the government? And if those who mine on Indian land refuse to pay, why should those who mine on government land continue to do so? And since we are obliged to protect our diggings, wherever they lay, why shouldn't we regard as our own what we have to protect?

"There is a great itching for privileges and a superabundant measure of independence," a harassed subagent wrote. "Complaints about the right of ground and this and that and other rights accumulate daily from both the diggers and the smelters and god knows what and when will be the end of it all!" By 1839 the system had broken down entirely, and by 1847 the government authorized the sale of public land.

In the spring of 1832 Blackhawk, Chief of the Sauks, returned from the west bank of the Mississippi, where he had been dispatched by the white man, to the east, and began moving northward in the direction of Galena. Galena had already had one Indian scare back in 1827, when some soldiers in nearby Prairie du Chien had invited the wrath of the Winnebagos by stealing some of their women. While miners and Indians had coexisted peacefully since then, there was a certain wariness that was always ready to be fanned into panic. As Blackhawk moved north, the settlers became distinctly uncomfortable. "I am convinced that we are not to have peace with this banditti collection of Indians until they are killed up in their dens," wrote Henry Dodge, who would eventually become governor of Wisconsin. "They watch from the high points of timber our movements in daylight, and at night pass through the prairies from one point of timber to another, and communicate with the main body which are in the swamps of the Rock River." By July panic had set in. Miners and farmers threw their household goods into wagons and set off for Galena.

"The little place was crowded with families pouring in from all parts of the mines," wrote Mrs. J. P. Gratiot, wife of an early miner. "The flat prairie between the bluff and the river was covered with wagons, the families camping in them; block houses were erected on the hill, companies forming, drums beating, and Gen. Dodge was busy engaged in organizing troops and creating order and confidence out of terror and confusion." By fall, life had returned to normal, perhaps speeded by one Colonel Strode, who, being convinced his townspeople were becoming careless, had muskets fired at midnight to sound a false alarm, to the disgust of all who spent their night cooped up in the stockade in terror without cause.

While Galena was growing, and growing fast, it was nevertheless an island in the wilderness, especially when navigation on the Mississippi ceased during the winter months. Residents received news of Andrew Jackson's election from a postman who agreed to skate up the Mississippi River from Rock Island, one hundred miles to the south, for five dollars in gold. From the very beginning, lead was used as currency. In 1828 subscriptions to the *Miner's Journal* were "$3.50 a year, payable in lead or cash." Ten years later, the editor of the *Northwestern Gazette* wrote: "There have been no transactions in [specie currency] of late, for the good reason that there is none in the market. It was rumored last week, but we place little reliance on the report, that a glimpse was caught of a piece of gold through the interstices of a long silken purse in the hands of a stranger. He was supposed to be walking subtreasury. The affair produced quite a sensation . . . lead is, at present, the main anchor of our circulating medium. It is not convenient pocket change, though."

In that same paper appeared the following notice: "Mr. William Baldwin respectfully informs the citizens of Galena and the mining country generally that he has reopened his coffee house. Between you and I, he has got some of the best liquors in Galena, and will always keep on hand beef steaks, hot coffee, venison steaks, tripe, prairie chicken, pigs feet and sausages, which will be served up in the neatest stile and in ten minutes' notice."

By the century's midpoint, Galena had grown from a rough mining town to a bustling city whose future seemed as bright as any west of the Hudson River. Twenty steamboats a week came up the Galena River from the Mississippi, depositing silks and fine furniture, ales and leather which had been ordered from New

York, Philadelphia, and New Orleans. When they left, they took away with them a growing list of manufactured goods and agricultural produce in addition to lead. By that time, Galena was supplying the nation with 83 percent of its lead. If the Gold Rush of 1848 had drawn off some of the town's miners and had moved the frontier two thousand miles west, Galena had gained more than she had lost. An 1854 newspaper reported "600 to 700 arrivals daily" with all boats and trains having "their full squeeze of passengers." She outfitted them to the jingle of her cash registers and sent them on their way. In the meantime, native sons were returning from California with new wealth to build new enterprises. In June of that year five excursion boats arrived simultaneously and a thousand distinguished visitors—editors, professors, governors, railroad presidents, ministers to foreign countries—swarmed through the town to see "such a place as no one could conceive of without seeing it." It had changed greatly since Dr. Newhall wrote those words. By day, its Main Street, a solid wall of four-story buildings, bustled with commerce: twenty-seven dry-goods houses; thirty-four retail grocery stores; twelve boot- and shoemakers; thirteen tailors; twelve cabinet shops; five breweries; eight hotels; five apothecaries; four watchmakers; six wagon-makers; eight livery stables. By night, it echoed with a gaity that came up the Mississippi with the sternwheelers.

As its wealth grew, to the simple log and rock dwellings of those who had pushed back the frontier were now added the pillars and porticoes of southern plantations, the grillwork of New Orleans, the clapboard of New England, and the straightforward stone houses of Pennsylvania. An aristocracy was developing, which included Elihu Washburne, who would become secretary of state and minister to France; Cadwallader, his brother, who was to become governor of Wisconsin, and W. R. Marshall, later to become governor of Minnesota. But the most cherished members of the community, and certainly the most colorful, were two of Galena's own: men who had come up the Mississippi on longboats and who had made their fortunes from its river and its mines.

Hezekiah Gear started out life in Galena in such abject poverty that when he left Alton, Illinois his belongings were auctioned off to settle his debts. Desperate, he seized the opportunity to earn seventy-five cents by delivering them to the village square in a borrowed wheelbarrow. Gear came upriver in a longboat from Alton in 1827, with a group that included Henry Dodge among its passengers. Penniless when he arrived, he staked his claim, dug his shaft, and built a cabin using logs he'd felled from a bluff, rolled into the river, and pulled upriver against the current by means of a rope around his waist. The roof was thatched with prairie grass and the floor was earth. Gear farmed and prospected, with little success in either, until the Blackhawk War broke out in 1832. He joined the military as a captain. When he returned, he resumed his digging. Too poor to hire a man to work the windlass that would pull the bucket of ore to the surface, he filled it himself at the bottom of the shaft, climbed the ladder to the surface, pulled the bucket up, emptied it, lowered it again, and climbed down to fill it. When he thought the mine-shaft was deep enough, he began to drift, which is to cut a lateral tunnel, in hopes of finding a lode. One day his pick broke through into a cavity. Crawling in after it, he held up his candle. Ore glittered back from every surface. Here is how his daughter, Clarissa, tells it:

"When the sight of this great wealth met his eye, he wept like a child, threw down the pickaxe with which he had dug to this wealth, ran home to the dear ones, mounted his horse, rode into Galena, and went into Farnesworth's and Fureson's store. 'Gentlemen,' he said, 'I have come again.' They, thinking he had come for more goods, said, 'Captain, we must have a little money, bills are getting large.' Father replied, 'Get your horses, gentlemen, and come with me.' . . . The three rode out from town, father never saying where. He took them direct to his mine, he descended, then sent up the mineral bucket for them; when their feet touched bottom, father held up his candle and said, 'Gentlemen, look up!' "

What they saw was one of Galena's richest lodes. Gear was generous with both his new-found wealth and his talents, giving Galena several of its public buildings, property, and his services in city affairs. His house was the gayest in Galena, home to a steady stream of distinguished visitors, and he was known as a friend to the poor throughout his life.

Daniel Smith Harris was as different from Gear as night from day. He, too, had struck a profitable lode—when prospecting on his family's farm while still a teenager—but it was the river which had captured his imagination and it was the river which would win him fame. He had seen his first steamboat as a member of the Meeker party at the age of fifteen; when he was twenty-one, he was offered a spot as a cub pilot on one of the steamboats that called at Galena; when he was twenty-five, he was not only a full-fledged pilot, but had already built his first steamship, the *Jo Daviess*. At that time, settlers had already pushed their way far up the Wisconsin, the Rock and the Chippewa rivers, but the steamboats had been reluctant to follow. The settlements were few and far between and sparsely populated. The channels were unknown. Why should a steamboat captain risk his craft? What others saw as a deterrent, Harris saw as a dare. He went as far as the farthest settlement, and then a little farther. On the Rock River, he was granted a lot in each town by the grateful settlers. Harriet Bishop, an author, was aboard the ship when Harris brought a shipload of "soldiers and soldiers' baggage, soldiers' wives and soldiers' children, soldiers' stores and soldiers' equipment, soldiers' cattle and soldiers' dogs" up the Minnesota River to a new army post called Fort Ridgely, dragging a barge behind. She wrote: "His careful, quick and discerning eye saw everything at a glance and made all his calculations with a lightning velocity of thought so that we struck no snags, collapsed no flue and burst no boiler; though we did tear off the guards, throw down the pipes and leave the cabin maid's washing of linen high and dry on a tree, which bent down to receive the line."

If Harris liked the challenge of unknown territory, it was nothing compared to his love of a good race. He earned the enmity of steamboat captains up and down the Mississippi for his fierce competitiveness. In one encounter, when he found himself losing his lead, he swung his craft broadside, forcing the boat which followed him to reverse its engines to avoid a crash. After a second near-crash with the same boat, Harris brandished a rifle and threatened to shoot the other pilot.

In the summer of 1858, after two attempts to lay the transatlantic cable had been unsuccessful, a third was scheduled. It was an event that was awaited with all the excitement and anticipation of a journey into space today. Fourteen years had passed since the first telegraph message had been flashed between Washington and Baltimore, and by this time every important town on the Mississippi could boast a telegraphic connection with the east. Keokuk, Fort Madison, Burlington, Muscatine,

Davenport, Dubuque—all would know the instant the great event transpired—all, that is, except the towns north of the Minnesota border. It was a source of humiliation and outrage to the editor of the *Saint Paul Daily Pioneer and Democrat* who complained that Saint Paul, was farther from Prairie du Chien, Wisconsin (the last stop on the telegraph line) than Prairie du Chien was from London. But it was to no avail. The news would have to come by steamboat.

Both Harris's *Grey Eagle* and the Packet Company's *Itasca* were scheduled to make a run to Saint Paul as a part of their normal schedule, but the *Itasca* would leave from Prairie du Chien, 65 miles upriver from the *Grey Eagle*'s starting point in East Dubuque, giving Harris's opponent a significant head start. When the connection of the cable was made on 16 August, a special edition of the local newspaper was printed in Dubuque, and the *Grey Eagle* left with it, her engines stoked to capacity, at 8:30 A.M. the following morning. By 9:30 that night, she had reduced the *Itasca*'s nine-hour lead to three. All through the night freight was discharged only when necessary and mail was hurled to shore *en passant*. Passengers were persuaded to stay aboard by the offer of free meals and berth, not to mention the excitement of the chase. By 4 A.M., with 50 miles to go, the *Itasca*'s lead was only a few miles. By Merrimac Island it was three-quarters of a mile; by Newport, a half; by Pig's Eye and Dayton Bluff, two boat-lengths. The passengers cheered wildly as Captain Harris maneuvered the *Grey Eagle* abreast of the *Itasca*, but the *Itasca* put her nose into port first. The race, however, does not always go to the swiftest. While the *Itasca*'s crew was putting out the gangplank, a *Grey Eagle* deckhand shot an arrow of wood, a newspaper fastened to its notch, into the hands of a waiting agent. The *Grey Eagle* had made the 265-mile run from East Dubuque to Saint Paul in twenty-four hours and forty minutes, making twenty-three stops and taking on thirty-five cords of wood en route. It was the fastest time ever made by a steamboat. Three years later, the *Grey Eagle* crashed into the Rock Island bridge, and sank immediately in twenty feet of water. Six people were drowned. Captain Harris retired from river life forever.

It was the Fever River (now renamed the Galena) which had given birth to Galena, by providing access to its lead mines, and now the river began to die of the very activity it had generated. As more farmland was put under cultivation, more mine-shafts excavated, and more timber cleared for the construction of wharves, the channel began to narrow. "What can prevent it being ultimately filled with mud?" asked a steamboat captain who had struck bottom while approaching the landing—a not infrequent occurrence. "It has little or no current and is constantly receiving deposits of soil washed from the sides of the adjacent bluffs." By 1860, neighboring Dubuque, whose own lifeline was no less than the Mississippi, was poking fun at Galena as "an inland town." Its city council suggested that the bed of the Galena River be plowed up and potatoes planted whereupon a wag in the council chambers remarked that the ground was undoubtedly too dry.

Believing that its future lay with the river, Galena had remained somewhat indifferent to the railroads, and in 1851 had refused to accede to the Illinois Central's request for a terminal on the west side of the Galena River where the business district was concentrated. Hezekiah Gear, who had been a champion of the railroad's needs and of Galena's need for the railroad, warned, "Gentlemen, you have sounded your death knell, grass will grow in your streets, you have ruined your town.''

The nationwide panic of 1857 and the Civil War—which had closed southern ports, dissipated steamboat traffic and drawn off miners so that lead production failed to keep up with wartime needs—dealt the final blows. The "queen city" of the Upper Mississippi had lost the twin jewels of her crown: the lead mining of her hills and the steamboat traffic of her river. Men and capital drifted away, many of them to a promising town with the curious name of "Chicago" one hundred fifty miles to the east.

Galena would have one final moment of glory. It had already given the country the governors of Wisconsin, Illinois, and Minnesota, its secretary of state and its ministers to France and Belgium. Now it would give eight Civil War generals and the Supreme Commander of the Union Forces, Ulysses S. Grant. Grant, a retiring individual who with his brother managed the family's leather store on Main Street, was little known in Galena, but was a natural choice to lead the Jo Daviess Volunteers because of his West Point education and his commission as a Captain in the U.S. Army. When he returned to Galena four years later after Lee's surrender, twenty-five thousand people crowded the streets to welcome him. In 1868, when nominated by the Republican party as its candidate for the presidency, he made Galena the headquarters of his campaign. The night after his election, a torchlight procession of thousands of his cheering, exultant townspeople, led by marching bands, wound through the streets of Galena, finally gathering at his house, where fireworks were set off. A vacant building nearby, purchased for the purpose, was also set on fire. It could not be said that Galena did not go out in a blaze of glory. It had enjoyed more than a quarter-century of vigorous activity and celebrity—first as a boom town, then as one of the most promising cities in the west. It would continue to prosper modestly, on the basis of local commerce, until 1893, when the nationwide depression would deal it a mortal blow. This time, it would not recover.

A visitor to Galena in 1856 wrote: "I have been particularly struck with the unique, wild, picturesque appearance which it presents, unlike that of any place I ever visited. It is built on and among almost innumerable rocky hills and ravines. From no point can the eye take in more than a part of the city . . . and when you reach the rocky summit, and look around you, the view is very peculiar and striking. The greater part of the city is below you, and you gaze down on brick walls, and roofs, and smoke and streets somewhat wide and rough and cluttered with rubbish, as well as marked here and there with massive structures and goodly edifices and churches and stores and shops; and casting your eye around, you see on every side tasteful dwellings built amidst the trees and shrubbery, or packed like eagles' nests among the rocks, with overhanging forest trees."

The view from the rocky summit has not changed greatly, but today the paint on the goodly edifices is flaking, the streets are quiet, and the river is a small stream, used only by an occasional canoist. But the rocky hills and ravines, and the "dwellings packed like eagles' nests among them" remain, drawing a new wave of settlers, not entirely unlike the old.

⊰ 6 ⊱

Everyone Thinks
He's the First

On the cold, rainy day in 1970 when Kathy and Jim Webster set out from their Chicago apartment for a weekend in Galena they had no idea they were taking the first step in a journey that was being repeated in cities and suburbs all over America. They were simply out to see the autumn color. Moving to a small town, as far as they were concerned, was not even a remote possibility. Kathy had grown up in a town of twenty-five thousand —six times the size of Galena—and, she says, "all I ever wanted to do was to get out." Deliberately, she had moved to Washington, D.C. for her first job, and when she married Jim, picked up and moved to Chicago with pleasure. Jim had grown up in Miami, and after attending college in a town of fifty thousand, vowed he would never live in a "small town" again. When they visited Galena, they had been married less than a year, loved their jobs (Jim, on the advertising staff of the *Chicago Tribune*; Kathy, as the editor of an Illinois Bell employee publication), loved their apartment on the near north side of the city with its fireplace and bay windows, loved the ethnic restaurants, the shops, the entertainments, the excitement. But something on the trip captivated them, and by the following spring they were spending almost every other weekend in Galena, staying in a tourist home for eight dollars a night. One evening, sitting on the front porch and sharing a bottle of wine with the proprietor, Kathy said impulsively, "I wish we could afford a place here." They were told that if they had $2,000 in the bank—almost exactly what they did have—they would have a down payment on any place in town. The next weekend they looked at six houses and bought the sixth: an eight-room, two-story frame house six blocks from Main Street with two acres, a brook, and beyond the brook, nothing but woods and farmland. The year was 1970; the price was $11,000.

"It was strictly a place to come on weekends," Kathy recalls, "and for the first year and a half that's all we did. But it got harder and harder to leave on Sunday nights. One night in August after we had showered and packed for the trip back, we were sitting on the porch looking at the full moon and listening to the crickets and I asked Jim what time we'd have to leave in the morning to get back before rush hour. From that weekend on, I was late every Monday morning. I think my boss knew what was coming before I did. Life seemed so much simpler here. You could cash a check anywhere—no one ever asked for identification. And you could walk everywhere."

The more seriously the Websters contemplated the idea of moving, the more preposterous it seemed. Both were in the newspaper business. Where on earth would they find jobs? There was only the *Galena Gazette,* a small weekly they were sure wouldn't have jobs for them and wouldn't be able to pay what they needed if it did, and seventeen miles away in Dubuque, the *Telegraph-Herald.* Jim sent a résumé to the *Herald* and received no response.

Kathy was convinced that, lacking any experience on a daily, there was no point in trying. They decided that whoever found a job first—any kind of job—would move to Galena, and the other would continue working in the city and come out on weekends. One day a friend in Kathy's office saw an ad in *Editor and Publisher:* the *Dubuque Telegraph-Herald* was looking for a woman's editor. "I didn't even consider it," Kathy says. "I just wasn't qualified. But the people I worked with bet me that if I applied, I'd get an interview, so I applied, and I did. It was the day after Thanksgiving, and by the end of the interview I knew they were going to hire me. The editor asked what my husband was going to do, and I told him the personnel department hadn't answered his résumé. He said, 'When he comes to pick you up, have him come and see me,' and by the end of the day we both had jobs."

Both took a thirty percent cut in pay ("my own fault," says Kathy. "I'd said in my application that I realized I'd probably have to take a substantial pay cut") and both had to buy cars for the trip to Dubuque. "But we really didn't have to tighten our belts," said Jim. "After all, we were newlyweds with no children and good jobs. We'd been banking Kathy's whole paycheck anyway. On Friday nights in Chicago we'd go out to dinner and a show and drop $40—probably $100 by today's standards—and we'd do the same thing on Saturday shopping for dumb things like candles and baskets. We just rechanneled our spending. The house became our entertainment. And the mortgage was only $100, compared to the $175 we'd been paying in rent."

When they moved in on New Year's Eve, 1971, their only worry was whether they would find compatible people. "Since we were always working on the house, we didn't know anyone," says Kathy, "and I wondered if we were moving to a small town where everyone would be old and staid. But when I told the one woman that I knew that we were moving, she said, 'You give the party, and I'll invite the people' and suddenly, all the people I had worried we wouldn't find here were right here in our living room."

No one knows exactly when the migration from cities and suburbs to small towns and rural areas of which the Websters and we ourselves are a part began, but rural areas were already growing twice as fast as urban areas by the early seventies. In the case of Galena, there was no latter-day Moses Meeker, no hint of fortunes to be made, no sense of a new frontier. Just an odd little town, a ghost town almost, where you could pick up a house for a song and be surrounded by beauty. Thousands of people passed through it each year to visit Grant's home or to go on house tours or to see the autumn color. If they liked beautiful old houses and history and pretty countryside, the trip was counted a success. If they were looking for the amenities—for country inns or good restaurants or things to do—it wasn't. Either way they didn't stay. But of course you couldn't, really, because how would you support yourself? No, it was not a realistic option. On the other hand, a weekend retreat was a possibility. Good Lord! At prices like that, one could hardly go wrong. So a house was bought and the weekends grew more frequent and of longer duration, and what was strange and captivating became familiar and finally necessary until at last someone said, "Let's do it!" and the plunge was taken. And then, as the years passed, others came because now there was proof that it could be done, or because life in the city had become intolerable or because life in the suburbs was no longer that different from life in the city and was therefore not worth the commute, each thinking that he was alone in his thoughts, that he had always been a little crazier than his neighbors, who of course would never do such a thing.

"Everyone who comes to Galena comes with two premises," says Dick Elliott, the attorney. "First, that they've discovered it. Second, that a lock should be put on the door to keep everyone else out." That's true. But on the heels of those two premises come two discoveries: first, that others have preceded them, and second, that it doesn't appear to have made any great difference. If the neighbors have come from the same place, they have not brought the cities or suburbs with them. The swimming pool planned five years ago is no nearer to ground-breaking today. There is still no PTA. The library is still only open half-days and still largely unused. The newspaper is still full of the doings of Eagles and Elks and still devoid of opinion. There is, in a word, no chic—radical, expatriate, or otherwise. Inexplicably, even truculently, the town has remained itself.

When Christopher and Jim Hirsheimer decided to marry, they were living in San Francisco. Jim, 37 and a bachelor, was a free-lance writer and photographer. Christopher, 30 and the mother of two daughters, was managing a small, chic hotel and working in a restaurant. They sat down and started figuring: $700 a month for an apartment ("Nothing spectacular, just an ordinary nice apartment") $4,000 a year for the girls' schooling ("It wasn't that we felt *our* children should go to private school—it's just what children do after sixth grade in San Francisco".) By the time they had finished, fixed expenses alone totaled $24,000—before the purchase of a loaf of bread.

"We decided it was paying dues to a club we didn't want to belong to," says Jim, "so we got out a map—

literally." Perhaps the northern California coast? "It was the kind of place where you went and did pottery and wore fisherman's sweaters and took long walks on the beach, and both Jim and and I had too much energy for that," says Christopher. "It would have been like dropping out." The Southwest? "I like the character you get with old places," says Jim. "The Southwest just wasn't old enough for me." Long Island? "We wanted a house and Long Island would have been as costly as San Francisco." New England? "We were afraid the parts we'd heard about would be too precious and the parts we hadn't would be too hard to crack." Southern Minnesota? Wisconsin? "It sounded nice. It had a ring about it."

They flew to Minneapolis for their honeymoon, rented a Winnebago and started going from town to town. They hadn't intended to look in Illinois, but somewhere along the way they'd heard good things about Galena, and late one afternoon, pulled into town. "That was it. We saw a river, a little red brick town, and houses on a hill. It was beautiful and golden, and we parked the Winnebago in the Middle School parking lot and sat and looked down on the town. The next day we looked at a house and put a bid on it. We'd spent thirty-six hours here."

During the trip they kept a notebook of all they'd seen and felt and done, and of what they'd observed small-town children doing, to show Frances and Verity when they got back. The entries: put pennies on railroad tracks, ride bikes, catch fireflies, go to Fourth of July picnics. The kids, remarkably, were thrilled. "They were the right age," says Jim. "No boy friends and no special friends. Plus they didn't have the freedom there that they would have here. We'd been broken into three times and a man had exposed himself to Verity at the laundromat. That isn't a reason to move, but it all adds up."

In six weeks' time they'd quit their jobs, disposed of their apartments, said their goodbyes, packed their belongings, and were on their way across the country by U-haul truck and Volkswagen with two children, a cat, and a portable TV set. In the middle of the desert, Jim took the television and hurled it out of the window. "It was one of the most satisfying things I've ever done," he says. When they arrived in Galena, the real-estate agent who had rented them their apartment invited them to a party. "The people were articulate and interesting, but it wasn't Bridgehampton or Carmel with madras everywhere you looked," says Jim. "You could feel the pioneer spirit. Everyone was working. There was a young vital feeling." While Jim worked on the house—one of those "houses packed like eagles' nests" on the hill overlooking Main Street—Christopher got a job as front-desk clerk at an inn eight miles outside of town for $3.50 an hour, working the 5:00 A.M. to 1:00 P.M. shift. Within a year's time they both had businesses of their own. Christopher had joined another couple (also former city dwellers) in opening a restaurant on Main Street and Jim had gone into the antiques business.

There is something about the town that makes even the most fiscally conservative, emotionally unadventurous person dream entrepreneurial dreams. To walk down Main Street is to want to meddle with it, like a parent with an errant and underachieving child. Look at that potential! Look at all those God-given gifts going to waste! All it would take is. . . . If they'd only. . . . Why don't they. . . . Hey, why don't *we!*

In part it is the availability of all those empty storefronts—the "massive structures" and "goodly edifices" that housed the bustling commerce of a nineteenth-century metropolis now serving a town of only four thousand. In part it is the lure of tourist trade, the "failure is impossible" syndrome. In part it is sheer longing for the amenities to which one is accustomed—a bookstore, a clothing store, a movie theater, an ethnic restaurant. But beyond all these is the simple feeling that it would be *fun*—and what have we come here for if not to change our lives?

Barbara and George Paxton came to Galena in 1974, but the story of their move begins at 3:00 P.M. on a Monday afternoon in August three years before. Having returned the night before from a three-week camping trip to Colorado with their sons Steve and Paul, Barbara was about to go to the supermarket to stock up on groceries when she heard the sound of a key in the door. It was George, a veteran of twenty-six years in the data processing business coming home to say that he had been fired.

"It was a terrifying experience," Barbara recalls. "Twelve men had had their jobs wiped out, just like that. And when George looked for another job, he quickly learned that they could hire two twenty-year-olds for the price of one forty-year-old. Our parents had worked all their lives for little gold watches and their retirement, but as far as we could see it wouldn't be there for us. That kind of security no longer existed."

They began questioning what their goals really were. Their experiences camping had affected them deeply. "I was a city girl and I thought I'd hate it," says Barbara. "But I found I really enjoyed it. We kept asking each other 'Why do we box ourselves in when there's so much land out there?' It was so *free*. The air was so *clean*. The children were so *happy*. When George got a new job, our lives went back to normal, but I sensed that he was biding his time. The wheels were turning."

The click of engagement occurred on an autumn

weekend they spent camping near Galena, which they considered "a dirty, rundown little town." They were standing in front of a vacant, four-story building on the corner of Main and Hill streets when Barbara said to George, "Gee, what this town could really use is a candy store like your Dad used to have." George said, "I'm going into the real-estate office." Barbara replied, "You're crazy." By the end of the weekend, they had put in a bid on the building for $21,000. "I couldn't believe all this was happening from one innocent remark," says Barbara. "We are *stable, traditional* people, *conventional* people. Security has always been very important. We weren't wealthy. We were just an average family struggling to meet our Sears credit-card charges. How could we even think about it?"

George's father, who had spent seventy-three years in the candy business, began showing George how to make small batches of candy on the kitchen stove, and pronounced him a natural. George, who had always before spurned his father's trade, found he was enjoying it. Though he had liked designing computer systems, he had never felt entirely comfortable persuading people they needed equipment which in his own mind was of questionable value. And now a special project was demanding eighty hours a week. "We decided that if he was going to work eighty hours a week with no overtime, we might as well do it for ourselves, and whether we succeeded or failed it would be our own. We talked it over one night and decided to go for broke," says Barbara. "We set our moving day for March 1, 1974, and when it came I was completely undone. I cried off and on all day. I couldn't look at the rooms before we left because of the memories. We moved ourselves to save money, and the kids rode with my brother-in-law in the truck, and George and I rode in the Vega with the dog and the bird and the plants. I was still crying when we got in the car, and our neighbors were waving, and George reached over and said, "I never loved you more than I love you right now."

"The move was horrible. The truck broke down and rolled backwards on the hills, and when the truck rental company put us up for the night in Freeport so it could be repaired it was like a reprieve—putting off the inevitable for one more day. The next day, as we came down the hill into Galena, Barbra Streisand's "The Way We Were" came on the car radio and I started crying all over again, and begged George to turn around. When we got to the store, there was no one there to help us unload because we were a day late, so some kids at the pool hall came over and helped. We wanted to pay them, but they wouldn't take anything. That night the four of us slept on the floor in the store. I'm strictly a Holiday Inn person, and there was no electricity, and we saw a rat, and the tenants upstairs were throwing pots and pans at each other. I thought, 'This can't be us. What are we *doing* here?'

"We opened the Monday after Easter. George started off with caramel corn and he burned the whole batch and the store was filled with smoke. I screamed at him 'I love my family and my friends and my security and you can't even make caramel corn!' When someone finally bought something, we didn't even know what to charge. We had been so intent on getting the store ready to open, we'd never worked out prices! I think we took in thirty or thirty-five dollars that first day, and we thought we were really in the bucks. I can understand why the banks thought we were crazy. We really were. We had no idea of what we were getting into. We were just two middle-aged people who wanted to change our lifestyle. But it worked, and maybe the reason it worked was the way we did it."

How Do You Do It?

The Hirsheimers' deliberate search for a good place to live is unusual. To stumble upon a place or situation (as the Paxtons did) or to gradually realize that the second home or cherished vacation spot has become first in the heart (as the Websters did) is a far more typical path to country living. If the Hirsheimers' approach was unusual, however, the stock-taking that preceded it was not. High prices coupled with a decline in quality are the greatest goad to reappraisal there is.

And so people ask: the pollution of the air around us, the muggings and rape on our streets, the traffic tie-ups, the train breakdowns, the depersonalization of the places we live by chain stores and franchises and housing developments, the fragmentation, the regimentation, the alienation, the *incivility*—is it for *these* that we pay $150,-000 for a house or apartment and $45 a month for a commutation ticket or carfare?

Of those who ask the question, some decide that it *is* worth it. They love the excitement and exhilaration and sense of endless possibility that are as undeniably in the air of the city as ozone, and that drift over the surrounding suburbs in the same manner. The job is terrific or may someday be terrific or at any rate constitutes too good a deal or too much security to give up. The family is there. Friends are there. Ballet lessons and Cub Scouts and buddies-since-second-grade are there. The house, after all the years and dollars of fixing it up, is finally the way that it should be. The tree planted when the first child was born is about to give shade on summer days. The crabgrass is finally under control. They will stay.

But others ask the same question and are not so sure. They wonder, "How do you do it?", meaning not "How do you get up the nerve?" or "How do you talk the kids into it?" but *"How do you make a living?"* But it is the wrong question because it can only be answered by asking another question: *"How much do you want to live in the country?"*

This is not to suggest that if there's a will, there's a way, because that's not always the case. But the kind of flexibility, and even more than that, the priorities exhibited by the Websters when they decided that whoever got a job first—*any kind of a job*—would move and the other would follow is what's needed to find work in a small town. It scarcely needs stating that perhaps ninety-nine percent of all city jobs don't exist at all in a small town so that that the person who wants to move there has to be willing to take what he can find or else create a job for himself. And so a journalist becomes a carpenter, a public-aid caseworker goes on an assembly line, a stockbroker becomes a museum administrator, a newspaper-space salesman becomes a feed-and-seed salesman, an actress becomes a waitress, and so on.

Others find they can bring their trades and professions with them. John Bookless, for example, came to Galena to wire a house for a friend when he was twenty-two and working as an electrician for a contractor in the Chicago suburbs. He never went back. He traded his electrical skills for free rental of an old miner's cottage, eventually bought a house and an acre of land for $8,000 at an auction, and continues to work as an electrician today, with more work than he can handle.

Sue Staron, who had been sewing for custom leather shops in Chicago, came to Galena in 1975 with $250 and her sewing machine, rented a storefront, almost went broke, moved away, came back, and eventually developed a clientele throughout Jo Daviess County and in Chicago. When she arrived in Galena she lived in the back of the shop. In 1979 she bought an eight-room house, circa 1850, with four fireplaces and four lilac bushes and a five-mile view for $20,000. It doesn't have central heating, but she figures her next couple of jobs will take care of that. "I have more job security today than my brother-in-law who works for GM," she says.

Dick Elliott, who used to be a labor lawyer for Quaker Oats and who joined a small, general practice firm here, says, "I probably wouldn't have done it if there wasn't an established practice to come to—although I know someone who did, in an even smaller town down the road, and he seems to be keeping bread on the table. The independence alone makes it worth-while. The practice would really astound lawyers in the city. There, you're always out scratching unless you're with a big firm. Here, no one feels someone is trying to grab work out from under him. There's a high level of courtesy."

In addition to those who change their jobs and those who bring them along, there is a rapidly expanding category of people whose jobs enable them to live anywhere. Gerry Rappaport is typical. As regional sales manager (thirteen states) for a jewelry manufacturer, all he needs is an airport with flights that will connect with the places he wants to go, and Dubuque is as good as O'Hare for that purpose. Shortly after Gerry and his wife Marianne moved to Galena, Marianne opened an antiques shop, a venture she had long dreamed of, but which she thought would have to wait until after their kids were older. It wasn't that she didn't want to untie the apron strings; it was that in suburban Stamford, Connecticut (population 109,000) where they had lived prior to moving to Galena, her services *as a chauffeur* were essential. But in a town of 4,000, kids don't need chauffeuring and Marianne is enjoying an accelerated independence. Now Gerry has a dream. "If we were able to make this business profitable, or perhaps get into another one, *I'd never have to wear a suit or a tie again.* I'd never have to wait in an airport, or make hotel or rental car reservations, or give another salesmen's seminar. My life and my schedule would be my own."

As trivial as it may appear at first, the dependence on automobiles that Marianne noted and that is part and parcel of suburban life often emerges as one of the unsatisfactory elements of the old life during the reappraisal process. It was for Donna Basch. Donna was a newly divorced single parent with two young children living in suburban Los Angeles when she realized that although her life had all the amenities and even luxuries associated with California living, she was missing the most important one: time. She liked her job as a neurological technician, but she couldn't progress in it without a degree, and she couldn't get a degree while working and raising two children. There just wasn't enough time. She reasoned that a small town would free up the hours wasted driving long distances, and would certainly be cheaper and more stress-free as well. "It wasn't a permanent commitment," she says of her decision. "Permanent commitments are bad for a single parent—too awesome. Taking one step at a time is a survival strategy." But the bookstore she opened six months after her arrival will soon celebrate its second birthday. A small town may seem like the last place in the world a single parent or, for that matter, a single person would want to live: couple-centered, poor job market, limited dating opportunities, uncomfortably high visibility, etc. But that view is based on the presumption that singles choose where they will live on the basis of where they will find a large pool of potential mates. It doesn't take into account that this may not be the top priority, and indeed, may not be on the agenda at all. Sue Staron, who was twenty-six when she moved to Galena with eight-year-old Jimmy, says, "You know, it's funny. I never once thought about the social life before I came here. I just hated the same thing everyone else does about the city—the noise, the traffic, the pollution, and so on. I guess I've always felt that if I'm supposed to meet someone, it won't make any difference where it is."

Glinting through the stories of the Websters and the Hirsheimers and the Paxtons and the others is a new attitude toward work, or perhaps an old attitude re-emerging from a long latency: work as a means rather than an end. Can it be that the years of flying from this place to that at the company's command, with moving vans bringing up the rear, are ending? Can it be that the quality of life has declined to the point that, like water on the sand-planet Arakis in the fantasy *Dune*, the most ordinary, unexceptional, everyday expectation—a decent place to live—has become the new prize?

While many of the people moving to the country today are content to live in close proximity to the land, there are others who, like the pioneers of old, are drawn here by the dream of possessing a piece of it. It may be ten acres or two hundred. In almost every case, they combine whatever farming they do with an off-farm job, or at any rate, a supplemental source of income, which is the case among the farm population as a whole. Few of them would call themselves farmers, knowing it is a title not to be bought, but earned. But if they are not "real" farmers, neither are they country gentlemen. It is the wrong time and place for that game and they are the wrong people.

They do what they can. Perhaps this year they will do no more than make the fences tight and tear down the rotting barn and plant a large vegetable garden. Perhaps next year they will put a field under cultivation and buy some chickens and a hog. It is not the progress, but the vision that counts.

When Brooke and Gary Williams bought seventy acres outside of Galena five years ago, they weren't sure what they were going to do. They had made enough money from the sale of Gary's tavern and package-goods store in Chicago ("We thought we were wealthy," Brooke says with a rueful laugh) not to have to worry about income immediately, and they are not the kind of people who plan out each step of their lives in advance anyway. "We were buying a county home," says Brooke. "That's all. If anyone had suggested that I'd ever see Gary on a tractor I would have laughed."

They spent the first two years renovating their large old farmhouse, tearing down outbuildings, erecting new ones, fencing, adding a driveway, and in general, bringing order out of chaos. But then the money began to run out. Thirty miles away in Wisconsin was Platteville, a pleasant college town. Why not open a pizzeria? It seemed like a wonderful idea. And it was, for Platteville, but not for the Williams. After a year of working seven-day weeks and leaving their two younger children in the care of the oldest, Brooke said "Enough" and got a job as a secretary for an engineering firm in Galena. A year later, Gary left, too, taking a job as a carpenter. And that is where they are today—from nine to five.

But their dreams, and half again as many working hours, are back on the farm. Each morning Gary rises at 4:00 A.M. to bottle-feed the calves he buys when they are three days' old, and repeats the process each evening when he comes home. The chores take two hours, and when the calves are ill, as they often are, there are middle of the night feedings of medication as well. "The original idea was just to raise a couple of calves to butcher, but I found it was something I could do without being encumbered with a lot of machinery, that doesn't require much land, and that takes a minimal investment. It just felt right." Their old dream of a country home has evolved into the dream of a more-or-less self-sufficient farm. The plan is for Brooke to continue to work, but for Gary to stay home and devote all his time to the farm as soon as he is able.

As Gary stands on the big porch he built around the old red farmhouse, and looks out over the swing he hung from the giant oak tree to the brand new pens where the calves bawl for their bottles, he says: "I wish I had it to do over again. We should have picked a warmer climate, certainly. And it's an economically depressed area as far as wages go. Seven years ago I paid two dollars an hour more to a carpenter in LaGrange than I'm making today, and I'm well-paid for this area. The back-to-earth magazines are always talking about trading labor and machinery—you know, he has a baler and you have a combine —but it just doesn't exist here because our neighbors are older people who are proud and who have never asked for help. The house is too big and too expensive. And I'd arrange to have an income. You need something coming in every month to play country boy. I rushed into selling my business and I almost gave it away. I should have kept it. And I should have checked the town out more thoroughly. But that's my fault."

Brooke says, "We've lost the stars in our eyes. You read about it and it sounds wonderful. It's not really that way. It's a lesson in survival. We've never worked harder in our lives. But if you want to do it, you find a way."

Moving to the country, almost without exception, means learning to live on less. That's never easy, but there are several aspects of country life that help. The mortgage, which generally takes the biggest chunk out of any paycheck, is often smaller, or even nonexistent. The proceeds from the sale of the old house in a metropolitan area can often handily buy two comparable houses in the country. Without a big mortgage to worry about, you *feel* richer even if your paycheck isn't as big, and that paycheck, whatever its size, goes a lot farther.

Entertainment, like the mortgage, can be virtually eliminated from the budget. You make your own. And that's not all you make yourself. Whether or not you're a do-it-yourself sort of person, you become one out of necessity; the so-called service economy is a city invention that hasn't reached the country yet. It drives you crazy, but it saves you lots of dollars. Status symbols also have a do-it-yourself flavor. They are things like the chair you picked up for five dollars and stripped and stained to honey-colored beauty, the military precision of your woodpile or your plum jelly. Thrift is more than a virtue; it has a definite cachet.

There are two other distinctive aspects of country living which deserve to be mentioned in regard to cost. The first is that there is a wonderfully noncompetitive and relaxed feeling to being together in the country that's like those first apartment days, when everyone furnished with travel posters and Goodwill furniture, and an invitation to dinner was understood to mean Bring Your Own Bottle. It's a feeling that's usually attributed to youth, but which should be attributed to endeavor, which allows no time for the calcifications of behavior and the effort that goes into conspicuous consumption.

The second is that the best things about life in the country—the pleasure of people's trust, the exultation of freedom, the surprise of courtesy, the joy of independence, the beauty of the natural world—are not only free, but a part of daily life. Is it any wonder that the great tides of population that flow and eddy have begun to move outward?

8

A Proper Distance

Rabbits and chipmunks, cardinals and bluebirds flee from our path as we hurtle down the hill. We are on our way to town, a welcome respite from the whine of the saw, the pounding of hammers, and the screaming of punk rock. My crew demands not minimum wage, but maximum volume and a free choice of records. "Look, Mama, a hawk!" says Kate, and sure enough it is. We stop the car and sit entranced as it circles overhead. Yesterday it was an egret, the day before a great blue heron. When we reach the paved road, the driver of each oncoming car waves in greeting. The first few times this happened I thought it must have been someone we knew, but drivers here wave to other drivers just as people say hello to each other when they pass on the street.

My first stop is the post office, housed in the eight-chimneyed customs house. I have come to tell the post-master that we are here for good now, but he already knows: a carrier saw our mailbox on his way to work this morning, and our first delivery is on its way. At the telephone company, things are a little slower. Mrs. Heim says that the man who must survey our land to figure out how to bring us service has a broken leg, and we must wait for his recovery.

At the supermarket I see Stella Brendel, who says to be sure and use her phone while waiting for ours, and little Michael Limback who wants to know if the boys are going to the swimming hole today and can he go along. The next stop is Lonna McDermott's, to drop off Kate for a day of play with other children. Lonna's place is where working parents leave babies and toddlers, where school children come to spend the hours until their parents return home, and where people like me, who simply have a project to do, drop off their children for a few hours or a day. It is one of those red brick houses way up on top of the hill, and the view is spectacular—a panorama of the town. Lonna says she has picked out our house with binoculars. Her house is serene despite babies in diapers crawling across the carpet and preschoolers playing with trucks and dolls. The epitome of the well-kept house, it makes me wistful, even envious, and I tell her so. "Taking care of children is all I've ever done," she says. "It's the one thing—that and housekeeping—that I really know how to do well." It is said with quiet satisfaction and pride, without a trace of wistfulness or deprecation. I yearn for her contentment. She quit school to get married, and had the first of six children within the year. She's a grandmother now, but I'll bet she's still in her thirties. She holds Nathan, Laurie's child, on one hip, nuzzling him, and says, "Wait and see. No matter how many kids you have, there's nothing in the world like it."

She asks me about our water situation, which has gone from bad to better. We have water now, but still no hot water and no tub. Dick wants to see if we can get along with solar-heated water alone. Lonna tells me she and her five brothers and sisters used to take baths in an old tin tub on Saturday nights—in the dark for privacy. "We were poor," she says. "I mean *poor.* "

Lonna wants to come out and see our place, but she doesn't drive and she's tied down with the kids. She urges me to try some coffee cake she's just made with sour dough starter from her neighbor Kathy Harms. She is entranced with the idea of sour dough: the recipe Kathy gave her calls for building it up so that you will eventually have four cups—two for the coffee cake, one to keep, and one for a friend. She offers me the friend's cup. The coffee cake is wonderful, filled with raisins and nuts and brown sugar, richer than a layer cake. As I leave, another mother comes and Lonna reaches out for the baby, cradling him and crooning to him.

The next stop is the courthouse, to pay the first installment on our property taxes. We have been so busy with the move that we are delinquent, and our names have been published in the *Galena Gazette*. The courthouse with its awnings and flag would be recognizable anywhere, even though it lacks the requisite setting of a town square, big shade trees, and old men sitting on benches.

Immediately inside the door, hard by the Pepsi machine, is a red sign with faded gold lettering that says "County Treasurer and Tax Collector." A disembodied finger points to the right. I present myself and my tax bill at the tall counter and ask the woman in the summer dress behind it how the check should be made out. "Just make it out to me," she says. She's the county treasurer. I make out a check for $854.38 for two hundred acres, a house, a barn, and outbuildings.

My errands are finished, but I don't want to leave. The town's animation has grown with the hour. Main Street is bustling with cars and people now—people shopping, people chatting, people hammering, people sitting on steps. The pace is neither brisk nor sleepy; the word cheerful comes to mind. A man in jeans and a T-shirt and a carpenter's apron walks purposefully down the sidewalk, sees a friend on the other side of the street, swings across, stands chatting for a while, then moves on, calling out a final volley as he moves back across the street. The street, like the walls of the buildings, is merely an interruption in the flow of things. I find my excuse to hang around a little longer in the library; I will stop to pick up some books for Kate before going home.

It is a classic Carnegie library: dreary, predictable, its gray Greek Revival facade dissonant in a town of red brick and white gingerbread. But inside it has that hushed and dim atmosphere that I love, which no plate-glass and lounge-chair library can ever capture. Those libraries are places of business, produced by the same people who design dentists' offices and motel rooms. *This* is a library—peaceful, enduring, seductive, mysterious—and a shade melancholy.

The library is as cool and dim and empty as the day outside is hot and bright and full of life. Paddlewheel fans stir the air, their low hum the only sound. In front of the window which looks down upon the levee sit five empty and motionless rocking chairs. Across from it is a large fireplace, with cloisonné clusters of wisteria worked upon its face. Looking down on the reading tables are marbles ("The First Lesson"), bronze busts (William Shakespeare) and a broken menorah. By the door is an old-fashioned stereoptican with a ladder up to its eyepiece for children. I turn the crank at its side and the sights of Halliburton's travels—a charging rhinoceros, a trumpeting elephant, a tribe of Pygmies—come alive before my eyes.

The library's works are eclectic, as if the books of a thousand summer cottages were gathered under one roof. There is no attempt to market its wares. It is just

here, like the town, for whoever finds it, and on this
particular day no one has. When the librarian learns
where we live, she apologetically tells me that the charge
will be six dollars for a library card: we are outside the
town limits. Outside the town limits? How can it be? I
love this town. Am I really not a part of it? It is the gift
at the bottom of the box, the one you find tangled in the
tissue paper after you've unwrapped the big one. I already know more people here than I knew after four
years in Evanston. I tell her our house is only three miles
away—actually two miles as the crow flies—look, you
can probably see it from the window. She feels badly, but
what can she do? We are just over the line. Oh, well. I
pay up and put my card in my billfold. I have a mail box,
a library card, a receipt for my property taxes, and a cup
of sour dough starter. What more could anyone want?

"Ready?"
I grasp the slats at the rear of the hay wagon for balance and nod. A lurch and we are off. The tractor pulls
the wagon; the wagon pulls the hay elevator, a towering
isosceles triangle on wheels. Running the length of its
surface are twelve wooden rods, each hung with innumerable iron fingers. As the rods move up and down in
squeaky rhythm, the fingers grab the loose hay from the
field and move it upward to the top, where it spills down
into the hay wagon. There is nothing to do but watch at
first; we are still on our way to the field where the rows
of hay cut three days ago make broad tan stripes against
the green. Standing atop the open wagon as it moves
slowly across the field I feel a giddy exhilaration I have
not felt since a child. Look, ma, no hands! I love the
motion, the pattern of sound the squeaking makes, the
slight breeze on my hot skin, the scent of the purple
alfalfa blossoms.

"Ready?" my driver asks again. We have gained the rows of hay. I position myself, pitchfork ready, and impatiently gesture him on. Who does he think he is? But I am more charmed than irritated for he is our oldest son, returned from a year of living and working away from home an almost-man. He has missed much. The snowbound weekends, the nights around the fire, the first dazzling wonder of it all can never be his, but he has claimed the giant oak tree on the ridge to fell, and the haying, asserting his part in this adventure, this family, still.

My job is to move the hay from the rear of the wagon, where it falls, to the front, and to watch for still-green hay which can generate enough heat to burn a barn. If we had a hay rake, I wouldn't have to worry about the green stuff. It would have been turned, and uniformly dry. We do have a hay rake, but it is beyond repair.

At first it is easy, even fun. Spear, lift, pivot, fling. The hay is surprisingly light. I watch for the green stuff like a hawk, using my hands to separate it out and fling it over the side of the wagon, but there is no time for such refinements. I am already behind: the hay surrounds me and keeps coming. In pausing to move it to the front, I lose still more ground. I have to call a halt. I rearrange it and begin again. But now the wagon, my terra firma, has disappeared, and I lurch and slide in the hay, trying to gain my footing. "Stamp on it," yells Harry from the tractor, but there is no time. Without solid ground beneath me I have lost my balance and rhythm. The fork is heavy, my knees are weak, and my heart is pounding. I ask him to stop. "Hey, mom, you know those seventy-nine-cent buttons?" He refers to the button which I wear on my purse, a green button with a white "59¢"—a reference to the fact that for every dollar made by a man, a woman earns only fifty-nine cents. He is teasing me for my fatigue. I point out that I am twenty-three years older than he is, and that it isn't seventy-nine cents anyway, but fifty-nine cents. He is so shocked by the greater discrepancy he is embarrassed. I may not be worth a dollar, but I am certainly worth more than fifty-nine cents.

We trade places and I drive the tractor for a while, grateful for the opportunity to rest, but I am soon accosted by panic. We are going along a gentle slope, and I have to fight to remain in the metal seat. I summon all the laws of physics I can remember to combat the sure knowledge that I am momentarily going to tip over and be crushed. I want to master this machine, but in my own time, on the level, without being told how easy it is and without having to prove my competence before I gain it. We trade places again, and again I fight for balance on the mountain of hay which now totally obscures the wagon. My wrists and ribs ache. Spear, stagger; lift, stagger; pivot, stagger; drop. I fall into the hay for a moment to rest, but have to scramble unsteadily to my feet before I am buried. Finally we are back where we started—one full turn of the small field, one load of hay. He turns off the tractor and goes to the elevator to detach it from the wagon. It will be left in the field for the next round while we go back to the barn. I wipe the sweat from my face. On his way back to the tractor, he tells me he was only kidding about the seventy-nine cents. He pauses, and thinks seriously about what value he would attach to my performance. He decides I am worthy of a dollar; I have done as well as Billy did on the last round.

Dick walks through the field to meet us, a can of beer in his hand. He's been in the barn unloading the last load with Billy. I've never liked beer, but that's because I never knew what it was for. It's for drinking ice-cold in the middle of a hayfield, your knees trembling, your skin prickling with hay and sweat, so hot you think you're going to die. We drive the wagon to the barn and leave it there while we drink another beer under the shade of the cottonwood tree. The shade and the cold beer feel wonderful, as does the breeze which drifts bits of white cottonwood fluff down on us.

Now we have to move the hay from the wagon to the barn floor. We work with pitchforks at first, the motes of dust filling the slants of afternoon sunlight that comes through the cracks in the old barn boards. Our barn was probably a poor man's barn, a friend told us. It is not one of those red, gambrel-roofed structures that adorn Christmas cards, but slope-roofed, silvery with age, and listing from the wind. Its roof beams are peeled logs; its ladders, straight branches cut from trees; its floor joists hand-hewn and a foot in diameter. Barn swallows nest in the cross-girders, and at the end wall, high up where the slopes of the roof meet, is a dovecote, filled with the cooing and burbling of pigeons.

Looking at the roof, we notice a harpoon fork hanging from the ceiling, and decide to try it. In conception it is an elegant contraption: horses are meant to pull the rope that lifts the fork with its load of hay to the ceiling, where it traps a lever that slams it across the barn to the farthest corner and drops it there. We have no horses yet, so we work out our own routine. I set it, plunging the tongs into the loose hay, then pulling the lever that makes them grab. Dick yanks the rope that lifts it to the ceiling. Bill, on the far side of the barn, pulls another rope that slams it across the ceiling to the farthest wall; then Dick pulls his rope again, releasing it to the floor. It's fun. It's also dangerous. The name harpoon fork is apt: it could as easily impale a man as a load of hay. The product of four days' haying seems small in the cavernous barn. We have no idea of how much we will need.

We don't even know what livestock we will have by winter. So far, we have acquired seven heifers. But it is enough for now.

We decide to go for a swim, and pile into the four-wheel drive, bounce across two fields, and down to the railroad track. Across the track is another field, woods, and finally the river. This part of the farm seems wilder, perhaps because the track creates a barrier, both psychological and real. It has not been cultivated or grazed in years. The brambles of wild raspberry and wild rose are waist-high, as are the stands of young sumac trees. Here and there are bottle gentians and brown-eyed Susans. The woods by the river are choked with trees: upright living trees, diagonal dying ones leaning in the arms of their neighbors, horizontal dead ones decomposing on the forest floor, and born-again trees, their roots exposed but their branches taking new life from the water of the river. Everywhere are vines, so rampant that it is easy to mistake their foliage for that of the trees. Nettles grow waist-high. It is more of a jungle than a woods, never fully dry because of the river, and in the mud we see the cloven, heart-shaped hoof of deer and the narrow footprint of raccoon. The mosquitoes have found us, surround us, and we quickly undress and rush into the river. The bottom is a revolting black muck that seems to have no end. We kick free and swim to the center, leaving the mosquitoes behind, but becoming prey to persistent deer flies. No one in Galena swims in the Galena River. No one I know anywhere swims in anything but a pool anymore, and there is, to tell the truth, nothing to commend this river with its mucky bottom, and its monotonous vista of trees, trees, and still more trees. Except that it is a river and it is ours.

Floating on my back, facing upstream, I see a great blue heron flying toward me, its long legs stretched out behind, its great wings heavily flapping. Kate, who is wearing a life jacket, is frenzied with excitement at being able to stay up in the water unassisted. She dog-paddles furiously from one to the other of us, turning away with a shrill "Don't touch me!" when she comes within arm's reach. The rest of us do not so much swim as laze. From the coolness of the water, the day is beautiful. When the sun drops below the trees, it is time to go. Back through the mud, back through the mosquitoes, back through the nettles and vines and rotting logs, up the hill to the field, the car, and home. Someday, says Dick, we will make a clearing by the river. Perhaps we will even build a log cabin there with the trees we fell.

When we return I can again see the town from the kitchen window gently blurred by the rising evening mist. I feel infinitely blessed by both country and town, for they are not separate entities, but inextricably related, each enhancing the other: the country giving grace and beauty to the town, the town giving humanity and intimacy to the country. The relationship is the same as between an island and the sea: the sea is transformed by the sighting of land; the land transformed by the sight of the sea. Today we live on suffocating islands, without a view of the sea. Eight million, five million, three million people crowded into islands, and then an ocean of empty miles. No one can fly across the continent, or drive down a country road with birds singing and the air full of the scent of wild phlox without experiencing a feeling of something gone wrong, a feeling bordering on betrayal. All that space! Then why . . . ? I suspect that it is *that* space, not outer space, that will once again become our frontier. For the frontier is not gone. It never ends. It consists of finding the proper distance.

❧ 9 ❧

The Pleasures of Thrift

If I had to choose two events as symbols of the country life—or more exactly, as symbols of the way in which country life is different from metropolitan life—there is no question of what they would be: the potluck supper and the auction. There is something forthright and companionable about both events that contrasts mightily with corresponding occasions in the city.

There are so many potluck suppers in a small town that local restaurateurs must tear their hair. Benefits, too. On a Saturday you could start out at a pancake breakfast, go on to a ham dinner, and end up at a spaghetti supper and never pay more than $3.50. The auction, though, is my favorite weekend activity. Each week when the *Galena Gazette* comes out, Dick and I can hardly wait to see what's listed in the auction calendar. This week, there's one near Elizabeth that sounds good.

We set off in the pickup truck, and ten miles outside of town find the first of the red paper arrows nailed to a fence post. We follow them left, then right, then left again, uphill and down, winding through back roads until we come upon the long line of pickup trucks and four-wheel drives parked on either side of the dirt road. Kate and I walk hurriedly to the well-kept white farm-

house set far back from the road while Dick parks.
"How's it going?" asks Hal Schap, whose grandfather
founded the tiny town of Schapville just down the road.
He sits at a long metal table like a registrar at a voting
place, boxes of file cards and ledgers in front of him. I tell
him we have acquired seven heifers since I last saw him,
and take the stiff white card he hands me. Number 243.
That means we are the 243rd family to arrive and that
there will be lots of competition. It also means that I have
learned to read the subtleties of auction advertising well:
there's a lot of good stuff here today.

Through the doorway to the living room where curtains stir in the breeze I see a dozen women dressed as
if for church sitting on straight-backed chairs arranged
in a circle. The atmosphere is formal, subdued, but tran-
quil, a low murmur of conversation, and I am struck by
the curiosity of entertaining company and having an
auction on the same day. Then I remember. An estate
sale. They must be friends and neighbors, come to dis-
tract the widow.

John Balbach's jovial voice in the distance ("Come on
now, boys, who'll give me five dollars for this job lot?
Well, now, four dollars then . . .") followed by the auctioneer's chant, fills me with an anticipation and urgency
impossible to convey. "Somebody give me four dollars.
Four-dollah, four-dollah, four-dollah; now five; now six;
now seven; now nine (I got you—you're in at eight); now
ten; fifteen-I-need–twenty; now twenty-five; now thirty;
thirty-thirty-thirty-thirty; I got thirty; now forty; thirty-
I-need-forty, thirty-I-need-forty, thirty-I-need forty;
somebody give me forty. . . . Okay, thirty to the man
down there in the yellow shirt. All right now, what have
we got here? A nice brand spanking new can of weed
spray, boys, and it's full. Dollah-bill, dollah-bill, dollah-
bill. . . . " It is the sound of the last All Aboard for a

departing train, the sound of the brass band disappearing from view.

I try several spots for visibility, but there is no gap in the crowd that surrounds the wagon on which Balbach stands. They are mostly men, dressed in overalls or blue jeans, clean cotton shirts, and boots worn to the colorless, shapeless texture of old shoes. Everyone wears a cap emblazoned with the name of a seed or feed or equipment company: Hydrotex, Purina Chows, Wyffel's Hybrids, CAT Diesel Power, Goodyear, Master Mix, DeKalb. Those who are not involved, who await Balbach's progress to the next wagon, stand in knots, arms folded across chests, leaning against trees or pickups or the side of the barn, talking.

There's no problem seeing what's being offered at the moment—a cardboard carton of sheep shears, currycombs, elastrators, and a broken bird house. The challenge is to get a look at what still lies on the wagon so that I can make a rapid calculation of whether we can use it, what I am willing to pay, what others are likely to bid for it, and whether I should therefore up my original estimate. Shall I stay here, where visibility is poor, or use the time to make a circuit of the other wagons, the furniture, the tables of china, the boxes of household goods before they, too, are obscured by the crowd that moves at heel with Balbach? I choose the latter, and tell Kate I will see her later. She is an old hand at auctions and finds in them her own pleasure—a weeping willow to swing from, a friend to play with, a dog to follow, a fence to climb.

The furniture is arranged in facing rows on the front lawn: tables, chairs, end tables, sofas, recliners, hassocks, rockers, beds, dressers, chests, floor lamps, a television console. It is a typical mix of Herculon and hand-crafted pine, or in the jargon of auctions, "household" and "antique"—and nearly all of it is occupied. An auction is for visiting as well as buying, and why stand when you can sit? As the women talk, awaiting the moment of the freezer and the figurines, the children play among them, using the mattress as a trampoline. A baby, left by its parents in a serendipitous crib, watches the maple leaves stir overhead.

I admire an old armoire of pine, check its sturdiness and the fit of its doors, and wonder if it might be within my reach. We have a dearth of closets, and even at a hundred dollars it would beat building one, but still, it is a luxury. We have managed thus far; we don't really need it. We do, on the other hand, need dressers, but I can't get excited about any of them. If that small, ordinary painted one which has nothing in particular to commend it should go for three dollars or so, I might get it. I am looking for nothing in particular and for everything. The auction is my K-Mart, my furniture store, my hardware, my five-and-ten. It is also my Saturday afternoon at the movie with a quarter clutched in my fist. It is not entirely true that I look for nothing in particular. I look for something wonderful. Call it a totem. It may be a chair unlike any other, a box of old Christmas ornaments, a photograph, a child's scrapbook of long ago. I will know it when I see it. In the meantime, I cast a utilitarian eye over the rest.

At the end of the row of furniture is another wagon filled with junk—not a perjorative in this case, but a catch-all term for the flotsam and jetsam of the farmer's trade: pails and scales and bags of nails; fencing and fans and garbage cans; bags of feed and bags of seed; chicken crates and steel-gates; coils of rope and brown soap; levels and bevels; axes, saws, wrenches, pliers, ladders, compressors, chemicals, fan belts, tires, tubs, tanks, chains, shovels, hoes, pitchforks. . . . This is the part Dick loves.

I see several horse collars and make a note to tell him when I see him. Bushel baskets? Yes, for sure. And for that matter, we need a new pitchfork. I run into Michael who has come here independently on his motorcycle. He tells me he has bought a box of old 78s for fifty cents, and is off again. The box is surprisingly heavy; each record like a dinner plate.

Dick joins me at the junk wagon. The horse collars are too small, but there are some tongues he can use, and the anvil he has been looking for. I tell him Hal Schap, whose father used to be a blacksmith, says they go for about forty dollars at auction these days. When the anvil comes up, Dick drops out at thirty dollars. I ask him why. "There are thirty-dollar-anvil days and forty-dollar-anvil days." He refers not to the consensus in the crowd, but to his own feelings of amplitude or thrift, urgency or patience: "How much is it worth to *me* at this moment?" I tell him we've spent lots more for less value in the past. He says I need instant gratification. I tell him it's seizing the moment. We're not really arguing about the anvil in which I have absolutely no interest whatsoever, but about the boat at the last auction—a once in a lifetime bargain, but not, unfortunately, in mine. It is too fine a day to repeat musty lines. The anvil is none of my business anyway.

On the ground beyond the wagon lies a loose grouping of cartons of books and toys and neatly tied piles of *National Geographics.* The books are mostly Louis L'Amour, self-improvement, and digests of novels, but there are also some children's primers, an encyclopaedia, a plat book, and three Bibles in German. I have never been able to muster interest in the book-as-object, and move on.

And then I see it. A long-necked, square-shouldered bottle, tall as a wine-bottle, sitting on a table of bric-a-brac, the faint blue of its long burial irridescent in the sun. There are other bottles of pleasing shape and age but I have no eyes for them. I want this tall, angular, uncompromising fellow whose name ("Simmons Liver Regulator") and origin ("Philadelphia") are announced by raised glass letters. A middle-aged couple approach the table and absently handle the bottles as they chat. I pretend disinterest and pick up some cookie cutters. Is their interest desultory? Or are they, too, feigning indifference?

I have seen such bottles with a six-dollar price tag at antiques shops—and I have seen them elicit so little interest at auction they were sold as a job lot with Chianti and Coke bottles. I decide uncertainly on two dollars, and *maybe* three. I relocate Dick, who now has Kate on his shoulders, and we go to the lunchwagon for a barbecue and Coke. Today's wagon is run by "Kay's Katering —Elegant Receptions and Buffets," according to the faint blue lettering across the open doors of the rusting white Ford Econoline van. A trim blond woman, presumably Kay, dressed in shorts and a cotton blouse, alternately slices onions and flips burgers on a charcoal grill while an assistant hands out cold grape and orange sodas into waiting hands from a tub of ice. Sometimes there are thick slices of homemade pie—blueberry, gooseberry, raspberry, blackberry, and rhubarb. No such luck today. We settle Kate on the grass with her hot dog and return with our dripping barbecues and icy cans of grape soda to the crowd now gathered around the furniture.

The pine armoire goes for sixty dollars. I feel I ought to have bought it, but the lust to acquire, which was so overpowering upon arrival, has left me. I decide against the small dresser with nothing to commend it, but find myself entering the bidding on a rocker which seems stalled at a price lower than I would have expected. Dick makes a face which means "Not again!" and I remember the pieces of the last rocker I bought which still lie in the barn at home. I hope someone will rescue me, and someone does. There are just the beds left now, so I anticipate Balbach's direction and take up my position at the table of the bottles. It is a long table where the functional, the funky, and the unusual intermingle: stainless-steel mixing bowls, a blender, a crock, cheap figurines, artificial flowers, a roaster, souvenir ashtrays, junk jewelry, a box of antique spectacles, a kitchen clock, a piece of Depression glass, and the bottles. How will he handle it? He is superbly attuned to us, this handsome, tanned man with the curly gray hair escaping from under a Stetson, its sides rolled insouciantly toward the center. He learned his trade as a seventeen-year-old at the cattle barns; today it's rumored he's a millionaire. But not to us. We are a traveling congregation and he is our circuit-riding preacher. Services twice a day every Saturday and Sunday and sometimes weekdays, too. Exhortation, advice, jokes, assistance, information, matchmaking. You want to give up the farm and move into town? He knows just the place. You want two hundred acres on the river? He knows that place, too.

A woman with pink rollers in her hair is engaged in a *mano a mano* for the Depression glass with a tailored woman who has the look of a dealer about her. Dealer ups her bid to fifteen dollars. John looks to Rollers for seventeen dollars. She shakes her head. "Come on, Mary, don't worry about Joe. He's not hurting." The crowd laughs and Mary looks at her husband whose face reddens with embarrassment and pleasure. The decision is up to her. She bids seventeen dollars. Her opponent bids twenty dollars. Mary shakes her head definitively. She's out. The mixing bowls, the blender, and the figurines all bring a few dollars a piece. When he can't get a bid on the roaster, he tosses the artificial flowers, the junk jewelry, and the kitchen clock into it, excluding the spectacles, the bottles, and the crock. Damn. That means he thinks they'll bring a decent price. He sells the pile for two dollars, briefly whispers to his assistant, and then turns to the crowd. "Tell you what we're going to do folks. We're going to sell these things on choice."

"Choice" is the Russian roulette of auctions. To the highest bidder goes the choice of which item on the table he wants. He also has the option of buying all, or as many as he wants, at the same price. After he has made his choice, the bidding begins all over again for what remains, and so on until everything is gone, usually, but not always, at descending prices. The problem, of course, is that you don't know what the highest bidder will pick. You can hang back and hope he has his eye on something other than what you have your eye on and that you'll be able to get yours at a lower price during the second round of bidding. Sometimes it works; sometimes it doesn't. When you count on that obviously knowledgeable man choosing that obviously desirable crock, it turns out that he's mistaken your totem for his own and acquired it at a price you would have been agreeable to paying if you hadn't thought you'd get it cheaper next time around.

The bidding begins, and escalates so rapidly I am sure the bidders are after the box of spectacles—an unusual item with good resale value. I'm right. Roger Parsells, a friend, carts the spectacles away. The bottles and the crock remain. Do I hang back on the assumption the crock will go first? I decide not to take a chance and enter the bidding at two dollars, but I might as well have saved myself the trouble. They're up to eight dollars while I'm still deciding whether to go to four. The crock goes for ten dollars. Now there are only the bottles left. I begin the bidding at one dollar, hoping to disparage their value. A woman in a halter-top bids a dollar fifty. Good, that will help to keep it down. Someone else bids two dollars, then halter-top two fifty. I come in at three; halter-top offers three fifty. Balbach calls for four and I nod yes. He asks halter-top for five. No. Four fifty? No. The choice of the bottles is mine for four dollars. I reach over for the tall fellow with the square shoulders. Balbach urges me to "take a couple." I laugh and tell him no. The highest bid on the next round is one dollar. Halter-top takes three at that price and others the last three. Are those the ones she wanted in the first place? Could I have gotten mine for a dollar? I will never know and I don't care. I have resisted an armoire, a junky dresser, and a rocker today. I have earned my bottle and it is worth every bit of $4 to me. For the truth is, an auction does not establish value any more than a price tag does. I have seen identical tall pine bookcases go for $5, $12, $15, $9, and $6 in that order. I know they were identical because I bought three of them and they now constitute a beautiful, wall-long, built-in bookcase. Instead, an auction teaches that value is an individual judgment. There is a profound difference between going to a store, seeing a price tag on an object, and thinking, "Can I afford it?" or even, "is that a fair price?" and having to figure out what you're willing to pay. That's not to say that such judgments are made in a vacuum. As in the case of the shelving, the fact that others are willing to pay more, or unwilling to pay as much, can color your own evaluation, but ultimately it's up to you—literally —to name your price.

Several weeks ago I bought a bread box at the K-Mart for six dollars. The next week Dick picked up three for a dollar at an auction. That only needs to happen once to alter your attitude and buying habits forever. Acts that have the smell of poverty or eccentricity about them in the city are sources of pride and pleasure in a rural environment. The auction is a symbol, if not the keystone, of the rural economy. It is a window to a world where recycling is the rule, obsolescence is unknown, and where there is a deep respect for material objects. The wobbly chair with the fractured leg is not an object for the weekly garbage pickup but for strong glue and a winter's night. The ladder may not have all its rungs but it has years of life left, and in the end will make fine kindling. The odd-sized storm windows can be used as a cold frame to start seedlings, and the plastic ice-cream buckets make fine pails for carrying oats to the horses.

I have come home from auctions dispirited because I spent too much—and because I spent too little, shying away at the last moment from a bid grown large only in comparison to those preceding it. I have had objects I lusted for turn to disappointments by the time I heaved them into the pickup truck, and others grow more pleasing to me with each passing week.

I lament the twelve-dollar hutch I don't need, have nowhere to put, and whose left-hand door will remain forever shut for lack of a hinge and time to repair it; the six-dollar wicker baby buggy which pretty bargain that it is, I have no earthly use for; the fifty oak-faced, zinc-lined hardware drawers for five dollars (what was I thinking of?)—all bargains, but all unneeded, unused, and therefore unloved.

I take pleasure to this day in the tall, Lincolnesque leather and mahogany rocker Dick picked up for two dollars, the bushel baskets at a quarter a piece, the room-sized rug for five dollars, and the floursack dishtowels for fifty cents.

I regret the horse-drawn cutter, its wooden runners still strong and sound, its brown velvet upholstery faded but intact, that went for $190 when we dropped out at

$180, because we would have used it and enjoyed it for years to come and will probably never find another we can afford.

I am glad, however, that I lost the old wood cookstove with its eight burners, two ovens, and warming drawer, its bright blue enamel and polished metal filigree, to the young man who said his wife planned to use it for cooking, whereas I wanted it only for its beauty and to warm the greenhouse on winter nights.

The woman who got the cutter, however, was another story. I had seen her at a previous auction, bidding with an abandon that suggested not so much desire as indifference. I resent that indifference, for it contaminates not only the economic process, but the feeling of camaraderie that often develops within an auction crowd. For the best auctions are a kind of Woodstock without music: the endless lines of cars fanning out into pastures, the glorious day in a glorious setting, the troupe of performers, the unending rhythm of the auctioneer's chant, the cold water from the pump, the sharing ("Does anyone want this extra set of drapes? I can only use one"), the courtesies ("That's a real bargain, miss" from the loser to the winner), and finally, the convergence of individuals of all ages and stations into a friendly throng.

We have come to the end of the long line of tractors and discs and harrows and hay rakes. "It was a real good auction. Thanks a lot, folks." It is Balbach's benediction. Dick and I pay the cashier, pile our purchases into the pickup, and head for home. As Kate sleeps between us, we remember: the one at the convent with the sixty-four sets of hairclippers and the long line of black trunks which seemed like reverse images of the rows of white crosses in the convent graveyard; the one where the ornate Victorian baby carriage brought $175 and the coffin a quarter; the one where the boys bought the BB guns that shattered the windshield of the Toyota; the one where the fellow asked the old man next to him what it was that he had just bought and was told "Durned if I know. . . ."

While Bill inspects our purchases ("Hey, that's neat! How much?"), I go to the garden and cut a spray of pale pink rambler roses for my pale blue bottle, and carry it to my desk. From downstairs comes the voice of Fanny Brice, alive, in person, in our living room, resurrected from Michael's box of 78s. The song is "Second Hand Rose." Balbach was right. It was, indeed, a "real good auction."

❧ *10* ❧

Chili Sauce and Other Choices

The garden burgeons, and like a pregnant woman whose baby has dropped I number the hours remaining. Zucchini the size of baseball bats stare at me reproachfully from a bushel basket, neglected not once but twice. Swiss chard, grown gigantic, challenges my inventiveness. Cucumbers crowd my windowsills. But it is none of these which imparts the sense of impending disaster. It is the fragrant tomatoes, their innocent, maidenlike blush of a few days ago now a sassy and demanding red.

Indeed, the first faint contractions of my labor have begun. The counter is piled high with pots and pans, their syrupy interiors already hardening to a fine, impenetrable glaze. The sink is clogged with skin of onion and seed of pepper; in each recess of the stove is the product of a vigorous boil. But across the room, on the long pine table, sit twelve glistening quart jars of chili sauce. My satisfaction is utter; my pride knows no bounds. I reach for a soft, clean dishtowel, shine them lovingly, and call for Dick and the boys to come and admire.

Who is this proud and happy woman? What happened to the harridan of the past three hours who stormed and wept and cursed, who swore she would never, ever engage in this atavistic ritual again? For the truth of the matter is that I hate to can, hate the endless, boring hours of peeling and chopping; hate the tumult it visits upon the household and my spirit; hate the precision required (a half-teaspoon ground cloves, fifteen minutes at a rolling boil) and the imprecision of my response (where in the *hell* did I put the potholder . . . the tongs . . . the funnel?). What is the point of it all? One might as well ask a fallen-away Catholic why he returns to church on Christmas Eve. One can isolate certain elements, but in the end it is a primordial response.

The elements. . . .

There is, first, the matter of thrift. Not the penny-saved-is-a-penny-earned variety, for the cost in time, in energy, and in good nature is incalculable, but the simple principle of using what you have . . . of *not wasting*. To buy a lug of strawberries from Michigan to can in Illinois, as many of my neighbors do, seems to me a kind of madness, if not downright masochism. But who can sit and watch their own cherries rot on the tree? Their own tomatoes grow soft on the vine?

If thrift initiates the labor of canning, it is far too pale and dutiful a notion to sustain it. No, there is sorcery here, too. I am beguiled by arcane texts and arcane tools, by chemistry and aesthetics, by the challenge of learning and the satisfaction of mastery. But above all by the vision of the perfectly sealed jar. Row upon row of them, lovely in their stasis. I cannot rewrite them, weeds will not overtake them, nor will they emerge hours from now, like the pots on my counter, to be done again. Nothing, not even the act of writing, has the illusion of permanency possessed by the perfectly sealed jar.

But why go through all that? Why not buy vacuum-packed, labor-free, nonreturnable, government-inspected jars off the supermarket shelf? Why not indeed? I have asked myself the same question many a time, all the more so because I *do* buy seventy-five percent of our foodstuffs there. What sort of nonsense is this? What sort of play-acting? I am no Amish farm wife, impelled by necessity or seduced by the common ethic!

Some will tell you they can because home-canned food tastes better—and it does. Others will say that when they can food themselves, they *know* the food is good (meaning wholesome and free of chemicals) and that's true. But there is more. Canning is transubstantiation—the transubstantiation of the most perishable and homely commodity, food, and that most relentless and repetitive of domestic activities, cooking, into something permanent and inviolable. Canning is conquering. If I have gone through the fires of hell, they are erased from memory the moment I stand back to admire. I have put a monkey wrench in the spokes of the treadmill; I have, however briefly, stopped the world and gotten off.

There is also the canning connection. As I taste Jeanette's raspberry jam and Brooke's blackberry jelly, as I call Kathy to ask, "How many minutes at a rolling boil?" and tell Christopher, "You don't have to sauté the onions first" I am participating in a ceremony of gender. I treasure the canning connection—the connection with women's experience of ages past, and with women of all different kinds of experience today. There are advertising men and used-car salesmen and generals who like to use a hammer and saw for the satisfaction of knowing they can perform a fundamental human activity. Tradition leads me to sink my wellshaft elsewhere, but perhaps the stream I tap is the same.

The trouble with all this is that I plunge into canning with as little thought as picking up a can of peas at the supermarket. I am an impulse-doer, and like the impulse-buyer, rarely consider the cost. Visions are my downfall —the freshly painted room, the ground abloom with flowers, the rows of quart jars standing in the cupboard. The vision will not wait, but the room is larger, the ground more impenetrable, the canning more difficult than I had thought. What was my vision becomes my obsession and my obligation. I am no longer a free agent, but in thrall—and weary, resentful, and angry because of it.

How to break the chain? You must learn to make choices, a friend advises. Your own inability to choose is the source of your dissatisfaction. She is right, of course, and I try it for a while. I will work in the garden today; I will not can. I will work at the typewriter; I will not clean the house. It feels good. I am in command. But it lasts as long as a New Year's resolution. Is my failure self-indulgence? A lack of discipline? Yes, in part. I acknowledge that. I want it all—the husband and the children and the career and the chickens and the goats and the horses and the friends and the garden and the morels and the jars of chili sauce—and what is that, if not self-indulgence, or indeed, downright gluttony? I do not have the discipline to say no.

Still, there is something that chills in the current jargon of "options" and "priorities" and "choices." It has too steely a ring to it. The intellect responds, but the intuitive self resists, for what is an impulse if not a message straight from the heart? Perhaps I have already made a choice, a choice not of the mind, but a deep-down, long-ago choice of the whole self, to embrace it all and muddle through, to relinquish purity of form for variety of texture. If it is not entirely a rational choice, then neither are we entirely creatures of reason. In fact, I sometimes wonder if the yearning for country things and country places is not, in part, an assertion of the right side of the brain, a shift of the thermostat from cool to warm, the response to a surfeit of detachment. The lives that some of us lead—lurching and sputtering and spuming—may be closer to what we want than any system of priorities worked out on the yellow legal pad or in the therapist's chair. And perhaps the energy expended in perfecting and refining them ought rather to go into toughening ourselves for the ultimate discovery that nothing—absolutely nothing—is perfect. Or to put it in another way, into cleaning up the syrupy pots on the kitchen counter instead of staring into the bottomless navel of choice.

❧ *11* ❧

Learning to Love a Barking Dog

Herman's barking pierces the still summer afternoon and my spirit responds with an inward groan. There is no question what the ruckus is about. Visitors—unbidden, unannounced, and unwanted. Resentfully, I jam my paint brush in the jar of turpentine and go outside. The unannounced visit is something I will never understand. Doesn't everyone want to know ahead of time that someone's coming? Doesn't everyone want to know that someone's home before they set out to visit them? The answer is no. It is a mystery that taunts my mind, but there is one thing I know: it is not happenstance. The unannounced visit is as much a tradition here as a phone call first is in the city.

Perhaps in these gentler, slower, and generally more civil surroundings calling on the telephone first seems a cold and formal way for friends and neighbors to communicate with each other. I've noticed that some members of the older generation eschew the mails in the same manner, preferring to pay their bills person to person. Perhaps those states of being which are interrupted by

the unannounced visit—solitude, concentrated effort—
are not so highly valued or closely husbanded here. Perhaps it is even a courtesy: no call, no fuss. Whatever it
is, there is no end to our visitors. We are visited by
farmers in search of acreage to rent and by hunters of
squirrel, rabbit, coon, fox, and deer; we are visited during a Saturday morning's slumber, a Saturday night's
dinner party and a Sunday afternoon's passion. We have
even been visited by a fellow who was looking for someone else whom he'd heard was visiting us. The man he
sought left shortly after his arrival; he, however, stayed
for three hours.

If rural visits are unscheduled, they nevertheless have
a protocol all their own. The object of the visit is never
immediately announced. Such openings as "I came over
to borrow your . . ." or "I wanted to find out if . . ." are
far too abrupt. It emerges, like an onion out of its skins.
I have talked with a stranger for a good ten minutes
before learning his purpose, and often I am not entirely
sure of it when he leaves. The proper duration of a visit
is equally mysterious, determined by a feeling for propriety known only to the caller. I know this because all
cues that it is time to terminate—from the whining of a
hungry child to a purposeful banging of pots and pans
—go unheeded. The visit may take place anywhere—
sitting at the kitchen table, standing in the driveway—
but work should stop. It would be bad form, for example,
to continue to chop onions or dismantle the tractor as
you chat, though with friends who are frequent visitors
it is okay, and indeed, necessary, to violate this rule.

Today's visitor is Cracker, come to see the team of
horses we acquired last week. Cracker lives down the
road at the ferry landing. There is no ferry anymore—
just a telephone booth and a few dozen flat-bottomed
fishing boats and houseboats tied up to sagging piers. It

is a dreary place, a place of rust and beer cans and weeds. Its sound is of cicadas and its smell is gasoline. We met Cracker when we launched our boat there long ago. He watched, plainly curious, as we took turns stamping on the bellows and the flat and lifeless heap of gray rubber became firm and shiny and downright insouciant. It is a boat that arouses curiosity everywhere, or perhaps it is that we do, for putting our faith in it. We bought it the year we drove to Central America. It made sense to have a collapsible boat for a three-thousand-mile automobile trip to the shores of the Caribbean, and it served us well.

We, for our part, were just as curious about Cracker, who as he watched, periodically whistled and shouted and waved greetings at arriving and departing boaters. This was clearly Cracker's territory. He appeared to be in his mid-sixties, and wore a baseball hat, a down vest over thermal underwear, baggy pants, sneakers, and carried a can of beer. His face was tanned and grizzled. We exchanged pleasantries, and asked where he lived. He gestured toward an asphalt-shingle cabin propped up out of the river's flood-reach by cut-up railroad ties. It was surrounded by three semitrailers without wheels, three rusting pickup trucks, a horse trailer, a stove, several washing machines of varying age, two cypress cheese vats, and a large number of fifty-gallon oil drums. We have since learned that Cracker has spent most of his working life commanding earth-moving equipment— cranes, bulldozers, back-hoes, and the like. It is difficult to imagine him in a job devoted to removal.

Cracker lives not so much in his house as around it. Sometimes you will find him on his outdoor sofa, its slipcover bleached white by the sun, listening to the ballgame on the radio that sits on the wringer-washer, and drinking beer. Or standing in the road, leaning in the car window, jawing with someone who has just come back from fishing. Or down at the water's edge, giving his thoughts on the transfer of a speedboat from trailer to water. When he comes to town in his old white Buick, he often has one of his dogs ride shotgun on its roof, but he has left them home today in deference to Herman. He reminds me of nothing so much as a grown-up Huck Finn—the kind of man who when he was a boy would have put dead frogs in his sister's bed and awaited the moment of discovery with suppressed but dancing glee. Indeed, he begins his visit this morning by telling me that the field corn is ripe for stealing. What is life for, if not for raising a little hell?

Dick joins us and we go to view the horses. They are not the horses of our dreams. *Those* horses were monstrous in size, perfectly matched, and when they moved (necks arched, manes and tails flying) so did the earth under the pounding of their hooves. These horses are certainly mightier than any saddle horse, but their manes and tails are stiff with burrs, their demeanor docile, and they would far rather eat grass than prance. Nevertheless, we are immensely pleased with them, and pleased with ourselves for having gotten them. We save the best to tell Cracker last: they are *pregnant!* Cracker is impressed. Dick puts them in harness and demonstrates why we chose them, driving them to the gate, dropping the reins, opening the gate, and calling them through. They stop on the other side and await the next command. They are, in the language of work horses, well-broke, as opposed to green-broke and just plain broke, and that, more than flowing manes and tails, is what we need. *They* will teach *us*. Cracker notices that their hooves are cracked, and tells us to make a poultice of red mud. We file it in memory, along with his recipe for cooking a beaver's tail ("First you roast it until it bubbles, then you strip the skin off . . .").

Herman sounds the alarm again, and we are joined by Mr. Dempsey, our eighty-one-year-old neighbor who lives alone in the Gothic brick house on the next farm down the road. He, too, has come to see the horses. He tells us he used to farm with horses years ago. Dick asks him if he'd like to take the reins. The horses weigh two thousand pounds each and Mr. Dempsey, probably less than one hundred. He thanks Dick, but reminds him that he's eighty-one and has had two strokes. The horses are nice, but Mr. Dempsey's heart belongs to Kate. He touches her shining red hair with his gnarled hand and asks her how she likes them, but she darts off again, oblivious to his question, and sadly, to his affection. He cautions us not to let her run around the horses, echoing my own apprehension, but it is like trying to contain a butterfly. Life on a farm is filled with hazards, and no one is more respectful of them than the experienced farmer. There is the rabid bat, cat, dog, or skunk; the rattlesnake coiled by the fencepost; the harpoon fork plummeting from the roof of the barn; the rearing tractor, the bucking chain saw, the chewing auger; the brush and chimney fires; the runaway horses; the dark and watery cistern. Already Michael has rolled a tractor, leaping from it just before it turned over; a girl his age was killed in the same way only a few weeks earlier.

After Mr. Dempsey has left, we offer Cracker a beer, and as we sit at the kitchen table he asks us if we know how Shot Tower Hill got its name. It is one of those soaring rock promontories common to this part of the country, for which I had always assumed a vaguely military function. No, says Cracker. In the cave midway down, the men would wait for a signal from above to set out the screens, and then the smelters would tip a vat of molten lead from the crest, and the lead passing through the screens would produce buckshot. Cracker's grandfather was a smelter, and gave his name to Bawden's Furnace, a settlement around an artesian well where they used to smelt lead. I drove by it the other day. There is a single house there now, built over the well, and a sign that says "Bawden's Furnace: Pop. 4; Elevation: 619 Ft.; Beware of Dog." When Cracker leaves, a bargain has been struck: Cracker's corn planter for some of our sunflower seeds when we harvest them. We are the first in this area to plant sunflowers as a crop, and there is great curiosity about them. Cracker wants them for his birds.

Keeping horses, growing sunflowers, the collapsible boat, the composting toilet—I sense that we are a source of endless curiosity to our neighbors. If we have come from the city and have bought a farm, surely we must have money. *All* city people have money. But if we do, then why do we live as we do? Our pots hang on nails, our sofa is sprung, we buy our furniture at auctions. Why did we decline to rent the land we didn't put under cultivation? What are all these books for? What is going on here? It is a never-ending serial filled with suspense: *What have they gone and done now?*

A half-hour after Cracker's departure, Herman begins barking again. This time it is Ray Leners, come to check on his hives. Ray and Jeanette are our neighbors; we can pick out each other's kitchen windows with binoculars across the stretch of farmland that separates us. The Leners live in a white frame house on the last street in town, with a big backyard where Ray grows strawberries and raspberries and gooseberries. Today, as usual, bees are uppermost in Ray's mind. He talks of them with the mixed admiration and disdain of a drill sergeant for his troops: "Do you know what those sonofabiscuit little buggers have gone and done? Those little brutes have raised *two* queens!" When he returns from the hives he tells Dick with some satisfaction that Dick appears to

have *no* queen, and suggests that Dick accompany him to
see for himself. Dick is not in his beekeeper frame of
mind at the moment, but Ray insists. He is fit to be tied
by Dick's indifferent beekeeping. Patiently, cheerfully,
Dick says that he will get around to it, that he only wants
enough honey for our needs anyway. Patiently, cheerfully, Ray points out that he could be getting five times
as much as he does.

No matter how much or how little honey we get from
our own hive, Ray will bring us some of his—and baskets
of raspberries and sheaves of beets and a gooseberry pie
from Jeanette and pails full of bluegills and crappies. He
is a master of good husbandry, this spare, wry fellow in
the porkpie hat who came here from Minnesota after
World War II and never went back " 'cause I couldn't
find my way out of them hills!" He watches over us like
a guardian angel. It is a frustrating, thankless job. He
would shape us up if he could, but he can't, so we simply
enjoy each other, because for all the disparity between
Ray and Jeanette's orderly garden and our rampant one,
between Ray's pampered hives and our neglected one,
between their tidy house and our chaotic one, we care
about the same things.

After Ray leaves we have dinner, and after dinner
Herman sounds the alert again. This time it is Stella
Brendel, come to bring Sweet William and Stars of Bethlehem from her perennial border for mine. It is twilight,
and she suggests that we plant them immediately so their
roots don't dry out. Perhaps here? I am tired and want
no more planting today, but there is no way to decline.
While I dig, she waters, and it is done in a moment. She
urges me to stop by and dig up some rhubarb plants the
next time I come to town. It is difficult for Stella to get
out these days. Her mother has been in and out of the
hospital for the past year and is currently living in a

hospital bed in Stella's living room. Stella and Bob, both in their late sixties, take turns sleeping on the couch so that they can attend to her nighttime needs. They arrange card parties (euchre and pinochle) to amuse her, repeat all conversations so that she will miss nothing, lay out shelled walnuts for her to break into pieces when making cookies so that she will feel useful, show guests with pride the rugs she used to braid. It is a miracle of love and patience that makes me ashamed of every mean and petty act I've ever committed. I asked Stella once, when I was feeling gloomy about something or other, how she managed to be always so cheerful when her life was no longer her own. She seemed bewildered. "Why Mama took care of me for so many years!" she said. "I'm just trying to pay her back a little." I thank her for the plants, but she tells me I must never say thank you for plants or they will die. She reminds me again that the rhubarb is waiting and is gone. There will be no more visitors tonight.

I will continue to groan when Herman barks, and to begrudge the hours taken from a hundred projects that there are not enough hours in a day or days in a year to complete, because it is the habit of a lifetime, and because I need solitude. But living here has made me realize that it is not the only need, or the most important. Without our visitors, our lives would be diminished, and we ourselves would be mere visitors to this place. Cracker, Mr. Dempsey, Ray and Jeanette, Stella and Bob—all are moorings. If our life, like our craft, is somewhat curious and bizarre, nevertheless it fits into the slip of Ferry Landing Road very well with these lines. Besides, there is scarcely a craft or crew around here that is not curious in some manner.

Renovation Blues

"My grandmother used to tell me," said Kathy Webster, cutting apples in half and dropping them into my big blue granite pot for applesauce, "that three moves equal a fire." By that calculation, I have lived through a holocaust, and the end is not yet in sight.

I am an orderly person. It is not out of preference, but a primitive instinct for survival, as powerful as those for food and shelter. I knew that living in the house while we renovated it—a neat, tidy word, mendacious in its disparity to the real thing—would be hard. I had read the stories of houses abandoned midway, of marriages destroyed. I also knew my own vulnerability to mess—the depression, the cold fury I felt toward those I loved—symptoms as obvious as the red eyes of the ragweed sufferer. But no one told me that renovation is like moving every day of your life, each oasis of order laboriously created at nightfall destroyed the following morning, over and over and over again.

I drove into town to get groceries this morning. When I returned, a wall was gone. The microwave oven is on the sewing machine. The rug is on top of the dresser and the stereo is on top of the rug. The refrigerator is on the back porch and the spatula is on the front porch, next to the can of Brasso, the bowl of marinade from last night's dinner, the badminton rackets in the Rizzoli book bag, the hairbrush and the operating manual for our tractor. But where are Kate's sneakers, found only yesterday after being lost for a week? My cigarettes? The can of stain I need for this morning's project? Where, for that matter, is a cup?

All I want is a drink of water. I find the cup on the floor behind the chair, an inch of milk on the bottom, a drowned fly floating in its milky grave. I start for the bathroom to wash it, but it's occupied. I go outside, circumnavigating the scaffolding, the cement truck, the piles of lumber, the sacks of ripening garbage torn open during the night, the blown newspapers, the mud, the debris, and arrive at the outdoor faucet, only to find that a hose is attached to it, screwed so tightly that I cannot remove it. I trace its serpentine loops, follow its many joinings, to the end of the vegetable garden where it terminates in a sprayer attachment. Not only is the water off, but I cannot untwist this joining either. I go back to the house and get a can of beer.

Today I am going to stain the molding that will frame the sliding glass door that will someday—tomorrow? next week?—fill the gaping hole in the kitchen wall through which chickens wander and bats fly. I take the strips of wood outside to work. The town with its spires, the farmhouse across the valley, the tree line that we know marks the Mississippi—all look ghostly in the blue, smokelike haze. Sweat drips down my face, getting in my eyes. The thermometer outside the lumber store read 106 yesterday. It was in the sun, but so was I. The flies have become monstrous. Muffled thunder sounds all morning, but nothing happens. The tension is unbearable. Kate whines. Finally, I can stand it no longer. I march her roughly out to Dick, thinking as I have every

day since we came here that she will someday tell a
therapist of the rejection that will be her earliest memory. How could it not be so? I *do* reject her, a dozen, two
dozen times a day. "No, I can't read to you—I'm working." "No, I can't play house—I'm working." "No, you
can get it yourself—I'm working." And finally, when the
work is done, "No, I'm too tired. Ask Daddy." And
Daddy says, "No, I'm talking to Mommy."

The boys have their first physical fight in years. As I
begin to make lunch in the makeshift kitchen we have
created in the living room, I cover each ingredient for
the salad I am making with a paper towel to keep away
the flies. The floor is covered with insect bodies, spilled
Coke, bits of food, pink and turquoise Play-Dough, saw-
dust, and plaster from the last demolition project, which
returns again and again like pine needles in April from
the previous December's Christmas tree.

Jan, the carpenter who is helping us, and who works
long and hard, usually until five or six in the evening,
leaves at three. The heat is too much. We press on. The
shutters which I stained earlier, after the molding, the
most wretched job I have ever undertaken, are stuck
closed, immovable. Disgusted, depressed, I go inside and
grow more depressed still.

What is wrong? Dick asks. Is it the kids? Is it the mess?
He gently takes me for a walk; I half-heartedly follow,
trying to be nice, but I want only to be alone with my
misery. We look at the old, horse-drawn hay lift he
bought last week. We look at the living wall of bees, eight
bodies deep, that have formed on the front of the hive,
ready to swarm. We look at the apple trees heavy with
fruit, saying, "Pick me, use me." It is all part of the
oppression . . . too much, too much. We are doing too
much. I cannot stand this feeling of never finishing,
never getting above it. Briefly, I achieve equilibrium, but

inevitably the sense of being overwhelmed, overpowered, returns.

But next year at this time, he says, we will be finished with all this, meaning the renovation. Then it will be manageable. Perhaps he is right. I don't know. It is partly summer itself that is to blame. I cannot stand the fecundity. I mulched the vegetable garden last week with deep straw, a thorough job, the kind I pride myself on. Already the weeds are as high and as full as the tomato plants. Does that not give pause? Weeds that were not yet born when plants were knee-high, as high as those same plants a week later? If the house is an Augean stable, the garden is nature run amok.

The list of things to be done stretches far beyond the summer, the year. There are fields to plow ("It's been let go so long that you might just as well be pioneers breaking the prairie," said a neighbor cheerfully); crops to plant and harvest; buildings to tear down and others to put in their place; equipment to repair; the orchard to prune; livestock to house; fences to care for. Meanwhile, all of the demands of daily life continue: pay bills, do laundry, get groceries, entertain visitors, celebrate holidays. It is a large life, complex rather than simple, and it has defeated many.

Dick glories in it. It is the "more" he has always wanted. You do what you can do, and when it stops being fun you do something else for a while. The sky will not fall in. I am not so sure. For me, the unfinished is abhorrent. I am engaged in a continuous struggle—against the mess in the house, the vegetables in the garden, the apples on the trees, the demands of the family. And yet there are a few hopeful signs, cracks in the pattern. I leave the dinner dishes on the counter sometimes now, and do them in the morning. I have stopped making the bed. My lists grow shorter in deference to my failure ever to come to the end of them. And sometimes, I brave the dawn without one. We return to the house and I take a shower while Dick makes drinks. When I emerge, a freshening breeze has come up and we go to the porch to revel in it. It is twilight now. The day is done. There is nothing more to do. The lamps glow invitingly in the house where the boys have smashed the flies into submission, the smell of chicken teriyaki rises on the grill, and everyone likes everyone again. And as I stand there, watching the barn swallows swoop and soar against the lambent sky, I know that it is, truly, the most beautiful place in the world, and I the most fortunate of women. At least until tomorrow.

A Tale of Two Hundred Acres

If the excitement of a city comes from a sense of the possible—from the feeling that something utterly unexpected could happen at any moment—the tranquility and peacefulness of a small town comes largely from a sense of the past. It is present in old houses, old buildings, and old people. It lurks equally in the place where the sidewalk has begun to cave in, in the stamped tin ceiling of the drugstore, and in the memory of its white-haired proprietor.

The past is different from history, as different as an aunt from a stranger. History is behind velvet ropes, sealed in glass cases, and contained in bound volumes. The past is accessible and familiar: it is the bullet hole in the kitchen floor, the peeled logs that hold up the barn roof, and the cistern out back. We are largely severed from history. We are connected to the past. Or used to be. One of the prices we've paid for mobility has been the disintegration of a personal past. Today it's likely to be scattered from here to kingdom come like so many shards of broken china. It lives on in memory, of course, but somehow that's not the same, for memory is solipsistic, and the power of the past is to confirm and integrate.

One of the nice things about small towns is that the newcomer can tap into the past as easily as he taps into the water, gas, and electricity. All you have to do is ask questions, and the next time you drive past the nameless knoll it will be "Hangman's Hill" and the next time you go past the firehouse you'll remember how the volunteer fire companies used to race to the fires and how the first one there got a keg of beer later.

Occasionally, you'll even find the past and history merging, like the time I set out in search of M. F. Truett. I'd picked up a book of early plat maps—maps of land and lot holdings—at an auction and there, where our farm was, appeared Mr. Truett's name. I decided to find out who he was. My first stop was the small basement room of the library which houses historical papers. It is a school-like room, with tall windows, high ceilings, yellow walls, and old pictures, presided over by Sue Wilson, whose job it is to help people find their way through the papers of Galena's past. Also present was Whitey, a local mechanic who is tracing his family's history. As I sat at the microfilm reader, Sue periodically read aloud to us from the newspaper on her own.

> Three Galeneans were presented to the Empress
> Eugenie at her last ball at the Tuileries on. . . .

She is interrupted by the arrival of an elderly couple at the door. The woman is dressed in a pink polyester pants-suit and carries a beaded purse. The man wears yellow trousers, a dark brown shirt, and white shoes. They are looking for H. A. Young. "I think he died in 1900," the woman says. Sue checks the cemetery files. "We have a Christian and an Eliza in Hanover," she says, "but no H. A. I'll put the Census on." She removes the newspaper account of the Empress Eugenie, and in its place appears the spidery script of the 1890 Census-taker. The man and woman are from Minneapolis. This is their vacation and they've spent it in courthouses and parsonages and small-town libraries like this, following the trail of their predecessors across Illinois and Iowa and Minnesota.

Whitey takes advantage of the interruption to ask me if I'm making good progress. I tell him no, but I'm having a wonderful time on the detours. And I am.

September 18, 1846
The Red Wing [steamship] came in yesterday morning from Montrose, opposite Nauvoo, and we gather the following news from the accomodating officers. A Civil War rages in Hancock County. The feelings of both parties are wrought up to a state of perfect desperation. Blood and vegeance are the watchwords. At the battle Saturday . . . about thirty were killed—four of the Mormon party, three men and a boy, and twenty-six of the Anti-Mormons. The Anti-Mormons are rallying from all quarters, threatening the extermination of their enemies. . . . Most of the troops called out by the state authorities to preserve the public peace, join the Anti-Mormons. . . . All the women and children had been sent out of Nauvoo, and were encamped on the bank of the river, on the Iowa side. All were in a state of the most deplorable suffering . . . and all were nearly destitute of food, subsisting on the charity of steamboats, and those whose hearts are not entirely closed against them.

March 4, 1870
A man from Fayette County, Wis., came to this city last evening in search of his wife. It appears from his story that on last Thursday night, she crept noiselessly out of bed, gathered a quantity of money, some articles of silverware and a gold watch, then har-

nessed up a horse, drove directly to Galena, where
she disposed of the horse and took the train going
West, telling an acquaintance that she designed to go
to Fort Dodge, Iowa. She is about 40 years of age, and
leaves behind her three very interesting children. It
is feared that she is deranged as no possible cause can
be assigned to her conduct.

February 22, 1870
A Bohemian woman attempted to fill a burning kerosene lamp with the usual result. Her house burned
to the ground and one of her children burned to
death.

Whitey asks me who it is I'm looking for. I tell him
about Mr. Truett. "He'll come," he says. "They were all
here. And they all went someplace else." It is as succinct
a summary of Galena's history as I have encountered. He
writes down "Truett" in block letters with a blue ball-
point pen on a white 3 × 5 index card, and says, "I'll keep
my eyes open for him." Whitey has twenty-five hundred
such cards, which he refers to as "my group." Sue has
told me that they extend far beyond his family; he also
collects names that recur frequently in relationship to
his family; others that have caught his interest for one
reason or another; and still others, like Truett, that people have asked him to watch for. Today he has discovered
that one of his group—an early miner named J. Rablin
—operated a hotel on the east side of Galena in 1835. Of
course, he points out, it is possible that "J. Rablin" was
not *his* J. Rablin—"J" could mean Jeremiah or James, and
even if it is John, there is still the question of which John.
In the crucible of such challenges the genealogist is
tested and the amateur historian is born. Whitey leaves,
telling me to "watch out for the streetcars" and so does
the couple from Minnesota. The room is quiet as Sue and
I sit staring into our microfilm readers.

John Quincy Adams, we are rejoiced to hear, is fast regaining his health. The Boston Courier says the venerable statesman attended church on Sunday last looking as well as he has for the last four or five years.

Whiskey! Whiskey!

I have received, and will be receiving, from Haun & Co., a large lot of their whiskeys, rectified by their new mode of rectifying, which I will sell to the trade, where six or more barrels are taken, at lower prices than they can bring as good a quantity from Cincinnati. All whiskeys of theirs sold by me I will warrant as good as any Cincinnati whiskey of the same age and challenge comparison.

M. F. Truett

My Mr. Truett! I read it to Sue and she is off—to the 1850 Census, to the county history, to the city directory. From the 1850 Census we learn that Miers F. Truett was at that time thirty, that he was a merchant, was born in Maryland, was married to Selena, twenty-nine, born in Missouri, that they had three children, Gertrude, nine, Mortimer, seven, and Hetty, two, and that a young woman named Harriet Truett, aged twenty-six, born in Illinois, lived with them. From the county history we learn that he was a member of the committee that created the stock company that built the DeSoto House.

I long to continue the search, but it's closing time. As we emerge from basement to sunshine, I ask Sue why she is doing genealogical research, trying to conceal that I consider it as reprehensible as wearing an alligator shirt. "It's like a puzzle," she says. "It's the most wonderful puzzle in the world, the only one that never, ever ends." But does it matter if the lives she is looking into are related to her own? "Not in the DAR way," she says. "Not as an achievement. But in another way, it *does* matter, because it ties you into history. When you start looking for an ancestor who lived at the time of the Civil War, the whole period comes alive. All that history that was so boring in school suddenly becomes fascinating. Like the Felts. They were the first family in Galena to have a water tank on their house, and when it didn't rain, the servants would have to pump water from the cistern up to the rooftop tank so it could be used. That's the kind of thing I love."

Me, too. And I love finding bits of brown crockery while digging in a flower bed, and an arrowhead while exploring a cave, and part of an iron kettle while looking for mushrooms in the woods, and initials J. E. carved into the hand-hewn timbers and "Cold Day" written under the wallpaper. It just makes life more interesting.

I might never have followed up on Mr. Truett were it not for the power company. It was running lines through two of our neighbors' farms and had paid them handsomely for the privilege. Bob Brendel told Dick that it looked to him as if the lines were going to go through part of our property, too. It's a funny piece, a kind of long, narrow panhandle that lies along the railroad tracks and is barely attached to the rest. Bob said it had been subject to dispute in the past. We decided to get our Abstract of Title out of the safety deposit box and look it over before approaching the power company.

But you can't look over a title any more than you can look over an algebraic equation. You must follow it, step by step, taking notes, drawing maps, concentrating fiercely. You must learn the language of rods and chains, and be able to see "the South part of the West part of the fractional Southeast quarter" as clearly as the view out your window. For several nights Dick and I pored over it; for several days Sue and I looked up Census entries, cemetery records, and early newspapers. The question of who owned the panhandle was all but forgotten. I was caught up in what Sue had called "the most wonderful puzzle of them all, the one that will never, ever end." Here, then, is the tale of two hundred acres.

In 1846, Congress directed that the government's reserved mineral lands in the states of Illinois and Arkansas and the territories of Wisconsin and Iowa be sold. There were more than eight hundred thousand acres involved, including the two hundred acres located along the Fever River in Galena that came to be the Brendel farm. The sale began at the government's land office in Dixon, Illinois, on 5 April 1847 and continued for two weeks. The three pieces which eventually came to constitute the Brendel property were sold on 14 April.

To Stephen Marsden, thirty-seven, who had come to Galena from Derbyshire, England, thirteen years earlier

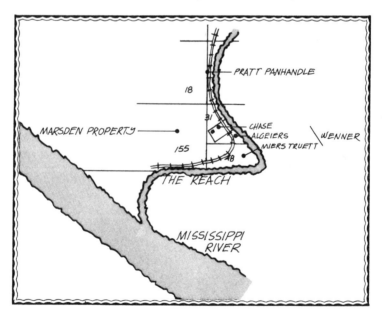

at the age of twenty-four, went the 155 acres lying along the stretch of the Fever River known among steamboat captains as "The Reach." Marsden and his brother Peter were mining prospectors whose nearby mines, the Marsden diggings, were already points of reference on the mining map. Within a few years the Marsdens would discover—on the opposite side of the river—the most celebrated lode of them all, the famous Black Jack Mine. The Black Jack yielded three million pounds of lead (some sources say eight million) and after the lead was exhausted, continued to yield zinc sulfide (Black Jack) until 1927.

To John Wenner, twenty-eight, who had been appointed township bidder to represent Galena's interests at the sales, went the seventy-nine acres adjacent to Marsden's property: a triangle bounded on two sides by the river. Wenner had come to Galena six years earlier from Lebanon County, Pennsylvania, via Saint Louis, where he had worked as a carpenter. He continued his trade in Galena, mining and farming as well, and eventually became treasurer of the township, a director of the school, and in 1850 the Whig nominee for representative.

To Orville C. Pratt went the eighteen-acre "panhandle" that lay between the northeast quarter-section line and the river. Little is known of Pratt except that he served as attorney for the Galena City Council in 1845, and eventually became a judge of the Superior Court in San Francisco.

In the Spring of 1847, when the sales took place, Zachary Taylor had just lead the U.S. forces to victory in the Battle of Buena Vista; a delegation of twenty Indians including the chief of the Winnebago tribe had just passed through Galena en route to Washington, D.C., to make a treaty for the sale of their lands; Dr. Livermore, the town dentist, was touting "Ethereal Vapor" for pain-

less tooth extractions; the steamships *Confidence, Uncle
Toby, Cora, St. Croix, Senator,* and *Lynx* were calling regu-
larly; twenty-four smelting furnaces were turning out
fifty-four million pounds of lead; Miers Truett's brother
Henry was mayor; and the discovery of gold in California was more than a year away.

In 1852, five years after buying the property along the
Fever River, Stephen Marsden sold it to a Michael and
Magdalena Eberhard for $1,600. The family Eberhard
had come from Baden, Germany, only three years earlier, and consisted of Michael, sixty-six, and Magdalena,
forty-nine, and five children ranging in age from twenty-
one to four. There was also in Galena at that time a Jacob
Eberhard, thirty-six, also of Baden, and his wife, Mary,
twenty-three, born in Saxony, and their three children,
all born in Illinois.

Jacob is listed by the Census as a merchant-tailor, and
we come across him later in the County History as having made, between one Saturday night and one Wednes-
day noon in April 1861, uniforms consisting of blue frock
coat and dark gray pants with blue cords for "103 men,
good and true"—Galena's first offering to the Civil War.
The age of Jacob's oldest child establishes that Jacob and
Mary had arrived in Illinois prior to Michael and Magdalena's arrival, and in the light of what follows it seems
fair to assume that Jacob had brought over Michael (his
father) and Magdalena (apparently his stepmother since
they are separated by only thirteen years) and his brothers and sisters to this country.

On 4 November 1869, seventeen years after Michael
Eberhard purchased the farm from Marsden, the abstract shows Jacob Eberhard filing a petition in the circuit court "for partition of the property owned by Michael Eberhard at his death," apparently because the
heirs could not agree on how to apportion it among

themselves. The court found all members of the family "each and every of them" entitled to equal shares but reported that the land was "so circumstanced that a division could not be made without manifest prejudice to the proprietors." An auction was held, and on 26 March 1870 the land passed to Michael Brendel, whose bid of $4,900 was the highest received.

Like the Eberhards, Michael Brendel had come from Baden. He had settled in Galena, gone to California for the gold rush, and had returned with enough money to set himself up in the ice business and buy some land. In 1870, when he bought the property, he was thirty-seven years old and unmarried. Three years later he would marry Christina, and they would have thirteen children. Eventually he would buy the property that Wenner and Orville Pratt had bought at the Dixon land sale as well, but that's getting ahead of the story.

When Wenner returned to Galena from Dixon, he sold off 31 of the 79 acres he'd bought to Edwin Ripley for the sum of $38 or $1.25 an acre. Ripley was an elder of the Presbyterian Church and the son of a banker. Nine months later Stephen Marsden bought him out for $300. It's possible that Marsden thought that the property might contain lead, but more likely—and this applies to his 155-acre parcel as well—that he thought the access to the river might someday be useful to him. Three years later, however, he sold it to John and Ellen Curley for $372, reserving the right of a road to the river from the house he had built on the adjacent 155 acres—our house!

The Curleys were from Ireland, and ran a grocery shop in the town. They got a good buy. Three years later the Illinois Central arrived seeking the right of way for its roadbed. After leaving Galena, the tracks would follow the Fever River, now known as the Galena River, to the Mississippi. It would pass first through the Curley's land, paralleling the river, then make a sharp turn with the river and pass through the Marsden/Eberhard/ Brendel land. The Illinois Central paid the Curleys $400 for a fifty-foot right of way on either side of the tracks —three acres in all. It was more than the Curleys had paid for the entire thirty-one acres. On the same day, the Curleys sold the rest of the property to John Towers, a tallow chandler from England, for another $400.

Now the price really started to climb. Towers sold off a three-acre piece of riverfront to a William W. Chase for $500. Chase had come to Galena from Vermont. He'd been a carpenter at first, and like so many other early arrivals, had flourished with the town, eventually owning a hotel, the Broadway House, and a livery stable. His obituary, in 1872, called him one of Galena's most prominent citizens.

But what on earth did he have in mind, back in 1854, paying $500 for a three-acre piece of riverfront property, two miles from town, with a railroad track going through the center of it? It's possible, of course, that having failed to reap the benefits of the Illinois Central's arrival in Galena the first time around, he wanted to secure property along its path in case the railroad decided to put in a second track. He may also have felt that the town was bound to edge its way toward the Mississippi, particularly now that the railroad had come, and wanted to be in a position to take advantage of future growth. But that somehow failed to explain why *this* piece—why this funny little rectangle with its short end on the river, intersected by a railroad, and sitting smack in the middle of Tower's thirty-one acres? In my concentration on paper property—on deeds and dates, rods and chains—I had completely lost touch with the land itself. I had forgotten the house.

The house isn't there anymore. You can't even see the

foundation. But it's right under the surface, ready to catch you when you're plowing and you can see it on the 1872 plat map. The house was situated almost at the top of a sloping field where it meets a line of trees. Behind the trees is a rock shelf that drops perhaps sixty feet. The trees are sugar maples, which are fairly rare around here, and lacy ferns and columbines grow out of the rock. Right where the house stood there are flowering fruit trees as well, and in the spring, spears of asparagus. Below the ridge, in the narrow field between the cliff and railroad tracks, is an abandoned well. Of course! W. W. Chase was willing to pay $500 for that curious bit of property that was like a slash through Towers' land because it had a house and a well on it! But who built the house? Probably not Towers, who had possessed it for only a year before selling it to Chase. More likely it was the Curleys. But if it was the Curleys who built the house and dug the well, were they, after all, pleased with the railroad's arrival and the windfall profit it had brought them? Or were they instead disappointed at having their homestead trespassed?

Three years after selling the three acres to Chase, Towers sold the rest to Peter Duffy, a grocer, for $1,000. That was a good deal of money in those days, and the land, now divided by the railroad in one direction and by the Chase property in the other, would seem to be growing less and less desirable—at least for agricultural purposes. It was bottomland, to be sure, but that is as often a curse as a blessing. During the next nine years—from 1856 to 1865—the land changed hands a number of times, finally coming into the possession of Genevieve and Dioneas Algeier who paid $620 for it. The Algeiers had come from Baden, Germany, a year or two earlier. Dioneas was forty-nine; Genevieve was thirty-five. They had three children when they arrived and during the next few years they would have three more.

The Algeiers appear to have had a hard time of it. On the same day that they bought the farm they took out two $100 mortgages at 10 percent, one payable the next year, and the other the year following. When the second payment was due, they took out another mortgage, this time for $150 for two years at 8 percent interest. Another year passed and they were back again—to borrow $400 for a year's time at 8 percent. They paid it off on time—with still another $400 mortgage acquired only two weeks before. This time the mortgage—whose interest had risen to 10 percent—contained a lengthy and grim rider detailing what would happen to the farm if they failed to pay back the loan. The loan was not paid. Instead, there was one last desperate transaction—$110 for one month at 10 percent. There are no further entries in the abstract until the sale of the Algeier farm by a trustee in 1880—ten years later—and there are no Algeiers listed in the 1880 Census.

I cannot help but wonder about those ten years. Were they years of unremitting dread? Or were there times when the corn grew tall and strong down by the river and it seemed that this would be the year they would get out from under? Was Dioneas a good farmer who had just started out with too little capital to make a go of it? After all, the bank had given him ten years before foreclosing. Or was he naive and ill-prepared? What kind of life had they lived in Baden? Where did they go after Galena? I am haunted by the Algeiers' story, like those of the "Hundred Neediest Families" at Christmas.

When the bank finally sold the property on the Algeiers' behalf, the man who bought it, Conrad Kraus, was the man who had given them the final $400 mortgage with the grim rider ten years earlier. He sold the property a month later, for only $2.00 difference in price, to a family named Dehing, who sold it three years later (in 1885) to Michael Brendel for $500. So ends the story of the thirty-one acres John Wenner sold to John Ripley for $1.25 an acre. But Wenner originally bought seventy-nine acres. What happened to the rest? Enter Miers Truett. Three months after returning from Dixon, Wenner sold the remaining forty-eight acres to a consortium made up of Miers F. Truett, merchant, Henry Corwith, merchant, and Alexander Young, attorney. By the following spring, Truett had bought out his two partners. In 1851 the *Weekly Northwestern Gazette* reported that "M. F. Truett of this city is to accompany his brother H. B. Truett on his return to California." Two weeks later Truett confirmed his departure with the announcement that "Alex Young is fully authorized to settle all matters connected with my business. Those who are indebted to me in any manner will call and settle with him and oblige—M. F. Truett."

Ten years later (in 1861) Miers Truett, then living in California, sold an undivided half of his Galena property to Henry Truett, also of California, for $500, according to the abstract. Another decade passed and then, in 1871, Miers signed a quit claim deed to "all of my right, title and interest" to the land he had formerly conveyed to Henry, in favor of Harriet Truett for $500. The deed, notarized by a notary public in "Helene County, Lewis and Clarke Territory of Montana," refers to Miers as the sole surviving son of Henry B. Truett, Sr.—telling us that brother Henry has died.

What's going on? Why is Miers turning his share of the property over to Harriet? Or is he deeding Henry's share to Harriet? Who *is* Harriet? And why is the transaction taking place in Montana when the deed itself lists Miers and Henry as residents of California? Could it be that Henry went to Montana, fell ill or encountered foul play, died there, and that Miers was summoned and executed Henry's will, or at any rate, what he thought was Henry's intent, by deeding the land to Harriet? But if the document represents a will of sorts, why is Miers charging, and why is Harriet paying, $500? Could it be that Miers needs money to bury Henry?

Whatever the answers, a month later Harriet sold her undivided half (for which, remember, she had just paid $500 to Miers) to Henry Corwith, one of the good ole boys who originally owned it with Miers back in '47, for $222.50. Perhaps the $500 she sent to Miers left Harriet short, and she turned to Corwith for help. But why only $222.50? And why not a loan against the property, if she needed money, instead of an outright sale? Seven years pass, and in 1877 Miers sold the other half of the property to Henry Corwith for $350, who then sold the full forty-eight acres to Michael Brendel for $894.20.

Now all the property is in the hands of Brendel except the 17-acre panhandle along the river in the northeast quarter of the section, which was bought by Orville Pratt at the land sale in Dixon. Almost immediately, Pratt signed a quit claim deed to the land "along with other land" in favor of one Hugh Birkhead and Charles Pierce for $300. Five years later Pierce bowed out, selling his share for $5.00 to Birkhead and Birkhead's brother, James, Jr. Two years after that, Birkhead has apparently gone bankrupt, for he signs a quit claim deed to an Oliver O'Donnell, requiring that O'Donnell shall "sell and dispose of the property and out of the proceeds . . . will pay all debts and creditors." For some reason this was never done. Perhaps O'Donnell preferred to keep the property and pay off Birkhead's debts with cash. At any rate thirty years later the land is finally sold—by the trustees of the estate of a now-deceased O'Donnell to

Michael Brendel for $180. The year was 1887; the farm as we know it today was complete: 155 acres belonging to Stephen Marsden, acquired by Brendel from the Eberhard heirs by sheriff's sale in 1870 for a price of $4,900; Miers Truett's 48 acres, acquired in 1877 for $350; the 19 acres lost by the hard-pressed Algeiers and acquired in 1885 for $500; and finally, the Pratt panhandle of 17 acres, acquired in 1887 for $180.

When Michael Brendel died in 1926 at the age of ninety-three, his wife and two of his thirteen children had already preceded him in death. The farm passed into the hands of Michael Jr., the oldest of the eleven who remained, who bought out his brothers' and sisters' shares. When Michael, Jr., died in 1950, the farm passed to his sons, Edward and Robert, and Robert's wife, Stella. In 1978 the Brendel line having come to an end, Edward, Robert, and Stella sold the property to Richard J. and Nancy Eberle.

A few weeks after I had pieced together the story of the farm, I ran into Sue at the library. She told me she had come across a new reference to Truett: *The People v. Henry B. Truett*. It seems that in 1837 Truett was accused of the murder of a Dr. Jacob M. Early, a hot-headed physician and preacher. Truett had shot Early in the lobby of the Spottswood Hotel in Springfield, Illinois, after calling him a "damned scoundrel, damned rascal, damned hypocrite, and damned coward" according to testimony at the trial. But the jury had not found him guilty of murder. It was said that the attorney for the defense had made a strong and sensible case, all the more impressive since it was his first murder trial. His name: Abraham Lincoln.

~ð *14* ð~

Progress,
Meet Self-Reliance

During those lingering hours of a party when drink or comfort or just prolonged exposure makes people intimate, the conversation here turns to the town as inevitably as it turns to children or marriages in other settings. I think it's probably because the feelings involved are much the same: affection . . . impatience . . . pride . . . worry . . . loyalty. Family feelings.

Our town. You almost have to live in a small town to understand what is meant by those words. Not *the* town —a neutral, geopolitical entity—but *ours*, ours in common, in joint tenancy, the town like a church and ourselves like a congregation.

And so it was that during the lingering hours of a party one summer night the conversation turned, as it always does, to Galena. More specifically, What To Do About Galena. As a newcomer, I found it puzzling, and annoying as well. Why should anyone want to do anything about Galena? It was wonderful just the way it was. I liked its seedy and somewhat rundown Main Street. I liked its redneck taverns and its raffish hotel. I liked everything about it that was unstandardized, unpackaged, and unplanned.

"We like it, too," said my friends, "but Galena's livelihood depends on tourists—or it should—and to keep tourists overnight you have to have decent accomodations, and shops that keep their posted hours, and things to do. Do you realize that business and industry pay only thirteen percent of this town's tax base and that in most communities they pay at least twenty-five percent? Do you realize that four more stores closed this summer? Do you realize that this town is in trouble?"

And so it is. I'd seen the hardware store close down since our arrival, the Coatesworth building fall down, and the five and dime and a clothing store and several others become terminally ill. And the town's attitude toward tourists seemed ambivalent to the point of schizophrenia. At one end of the spectrum were those who enjoyed sharing it so much they had to restrain themselves from buttonholing strangers and saying, "Have you seen the . . . ?" At the other end were those who, on the Monday after the Boy Scout Pilgrimage (when five thousand Boy Scouts spend so much money that bank deposits that day are at one of the year's highs) say, "Thank God that's over!"

My favorite story about Galena's love-hate relationship with tourists is the story of producer Norman Jewison's stopover in town several years ago to shoot scenes for the film *Gaily, Gaily,* a story of Ben Hecht's life. Jewison employed a hundred local people as extras, so the story goes, and paid each of them a hundred dollars, but when a local merchant was asked what he thought of it all, he responded huffily, "Mr. Jewison didn't come down *here* and buy anything! None of those Hollywood people came down here and bought anything! They just took up all the parking spaces!"

As far as shopping goes, what my friends say is true. Once you get beyond such fundamentals as groceries and a drugstore, you're in big trouble. Drab merchandise, inadequate choice and noncompetitive prices drive a lot of Galena people to Dubuque to shop, which of course means still less volume and still higher prices in a vicious circle.

"What this town needs," say my friends, warming to their subject, "is someone who would . . . " and they then go on to describe a brilliant, public-spirited man of vision who would whip this town into a midwestern semblance of Williamsburg. Which is passing strange, because that's exactly what it got ten years ago.

Robert Buehler came to Galena in 1959 in search of a place in the country. He wanted to be far enough from Chicago and his job as president of a large corporation that he would be difficult to reach, but close enough that he could go back and forth when necessary. But he wanted something else, something he calls "depth." "I wanted a place that wasn't just a pretty pocket. I wanted something that covered a hundred square miles— a place where I could go out for a walk or a ride and not find myself out of it right away." He found it in Jo Daviess County.

A little while after settling in, Buehler learned that there was no summer program for the children of the town. He had developed an athletic program for boys in Chicago which had changed lives. Why not start one here? The parents were delighted, and Buehler soon found himself asked to be mayor of Galena. "I realize now they couldn't find anyone else," he says wryly. "The local people were too smart to take the job."

After his election he plunged into a whirlwind self-education effort, reading and attending seminars on municipal government. At one of those seminars he met the head of Housing and Urban Development (HUD) for the Great Lakes region, who told him that HUD money might be available for assessing "whether it was feasible" to preserve Galena. Shortly later HUD announced it would finance eighty percent of the cost of qualified rehabilitation projects leading to historic preservation. Meanwhile, the state passed a statute permitting towns to have historical zoning ordinances.

Buehler might not have known much about municipal government, but he knew opportunity when it knocked on the door. He registered the entire town with both state and federal government as an historic site, got $125,-000 from HUD for a feasibility study, hired a planning commission, and established a citizen advisory committee and a parks and recreation committee. The objective of the study was to determine whether urban renewal techniques could be used to revitalize downtown Galena, which, like many small towns, seemed likely to lose its already foundering retail business to the nearest city or to a peripheral shopping center, and its buildings to the ravages of time. Specifically, the study would determine the history, condition, and restorability of each of Galena's downtown buildings; suggest directions and parameters for the restoration effort (should there be a new shopping area? was more parking needed?); determine whether, if Galena were restored, there would be enough business to support it; and finally, cost out the recommendations.

At the $62,000 point in the $125,000 study, Buehler changed planning agencies on the grounds that the study wasn't moving along fast enough: too much time, he thought, was being spent on analysis of what was, and too little on what might be. At the same time he started having trouble with the City Council and the city managers. "The two men I'd wanted on the council with me weren't elected, and I ended up with a couple of guys who weren't entirely on my side. Neither were the city managers. [There were two involved.] I also had a bad habit of running off on trips, which left the City Council to scheme, so we were in trouble before we ever got the plan from the planning people, and when we got it we were in even deeper trouble."

When Buehler talks about trips he's not talking about a weekend in New York or a week in Aspen. He's talking about two weeks in England or three in France. He's talking about attending seminars on techniques of preserving historic buildings; conferences on parks and open spaces; taking tours of rehabilitated city centers. "Just imagine," he says, still excited by the possibilities ten years later, "if we built pathways through the ravines and you could walk *all over town* without ever having to walk on a street. . . . Imagine a skating pond and a toboggan run and a short ski slope *right in town!*"

The conclusions of the feasibility study were predictable and noncontroversial. They were also typical of the problems faced by small towns all over America: the town didn't provide adequate goods and services to its residents; if the situation didn't improve "the present and growing level of unsatisfied demand is likely to engender a peripheral shopping center"; if that should happen, the competitive advantage would be so great that much of the existing market would be drawn away from downtown. As a corollary to all this, the study noted, the downtown (which in virtually all communities subsidizes, along with industry, the residential areas) had failed to provide its fair share of the tax base. When this happened, the study continued, there were two alternatives: either property owners were highly taxed for the improvements and services they required, or, as had happened in Galena, they went without "those public improvements and services that they should be receiving by any common standard."

The solution proposed by the study was to clear space for a few major commercial ventures—a supermarket, a variety store, and a top-quality motel were those mentioned—which could not, because of their specialized needs, be satisfactorily housed in the existing nineteenth-century structures. The clearance, limited though it would be, would not only revitalize the downtown area by providing new shopping, but would relieve Galena of some of the excess commercial space that had plagued it since its population had dropped from a nineteenth-century peak of fourteen thousand to its present-day four thousand. Specifically, the plan called for preserving and restoring the main portion of the curved, four-block-long wall of nineteenth-century buildings that gives Main Street its historic and architectural significance, but demolishing the deteriorating and historically insignificant buildings at either end. The new supermarket would go at one end and tourist accomodations at the other. The cost would be two million dollars. The federal share would be three-quarters; and the local share one-quarter. According to the planners, half of the local share could be paid by the city over a five-year period in the form of improvements to lighting, storm sewers, water mains and streets, and a significant portion of the remainder could be expected to come from the state in the form of grants for specific projects. Property-owners along Main Street would qualify for twenty-year, three percent interest loans for rehabilitation. Furthermore, the city might choose to take advantage of a brand-new HUD program for such major projects as the restoration of the historic DeSoto House Hotel. This program provided for cities to purchase historic properties, renovate them with federal funds, and then sell them back to private purchasers at fair market value, the only stipulation being that they be made available for public viewing on a reasonable, periodic basis.

More than two years had been spent on the Galena study, and several of the top urban-planners in the country had been involved, for while the project was a small one and the fees modest, the prestige was high. Two hundred and twenty-seven buildings had been punched and poked from their cellars to their rooftops and analyzed from an historic, architectural, structural, and functional point of view. Probably never before had so small a town been given such big-time treatment, which, hindsight informs, was probably a mistake.

"A couple of people with buildings at the end of town where the shopping area was going to be became very disturbed that their buildings were going to be torn down," says Buehler. "The word went out that what Buehler was trying to do with his urban renewal program was to buy up the whole area and redevelop it for his own profit. Well, I wasn't kissing babies and I wasn't going to funerals and I didn't appear in church and I wasn't hitting all those taverns, so there were a lot of people who believed it. As for the council, they were scared to death that the town was going to be responsible for the cost of the program and that they would have to raise taxes. Two of the five council members and the city manager were in sympathy with the opposition. The tavern people were mad because I'd tried to enforce an ordinance which was passed before I ever came to Galena that said that no new liquor licenses would be given out until the number of taverns was reduced to twelve. There were about seventeen or eighteen then. So Buehler was against all progress, against the little people. And the people who *should* have been for it—the merchants and professional people—wouldn't commit themselves. Some of them even said, 'We'll give you money to promote it, but we don't want to become involved.' It was like New York or Chicago where someone gets beaten up on the street while everyone else watches. In a short time the attitude had become 'What can a fellow from outside tell us about this town? We live here. We know what it needs. We don't want federal money. We'll do it ourselves.' "

One of the early urban transplants remembers it well: "If he'd been standing on a corner handing out ten-dollar bills, they wouldn't have taken one. They knew that if they'd had Buehler's money, *they* certainly wouldn't have spent it on the town, and therefore they didn't believe he was real. The poor guy—he had boots wiped all over him. The meeting at which the planners described the plan was really violent. The planning people stayed calm, but at the end they told them, 'You know, without The Wall—that's the wall of buildings along Main Street—you're just one more small dirty town like all the rest.' And it's true."

Buehler resumes: "The HUD people finally said, 'Look, we're beginning to run out of money. There's only X amount of dollars left in this fund and there are hundreds of communities after it. If we want to get in there, we're going to have to move pretty fast. We'd like the city to prepare a formal request. Then we'll put aside two million dollars and you can do what you want with it, because you're not bound by the plan. HUD gets approval but it can't tell you what to do. The decisions must be made by the City Council.' They suggested that the city pay the planning agency to write up the request out of its own funds, because if we waited for money from the federal government for that, the money in Washington that we wanted would have dried up. However the council said, 'If we spend our money on this request, how do we know we'll get it back?' So I said, 'Well, you *don't* know that you're going to get it back, but you *do* know that there'll be two million dollars available to fix up downtown.' They said, 'Well, we don't know. That's kind of risky. We might lose our money.' Actually, I think it was an alibi as much as anything, a way out. So they decided to have a referendum on the plan. That's when the opposition really went to town. They published a newspaper and did door-to-door campaigning. They went all out and they were quite effective."

The handsome, three-color, thirty-two page document titled "Preservation of Downtown Galena: An Urban Renewal Feasibility Study" opens with these words: "The question of whether it would be feasible to employ urban renewal in improving and preserving downtown Galena must be divided into three parts: Is it physically feasible? Is it financially feasible? Is it politically and socially feasible? The first two of these questions may be answered by the feasibility survey, but the third must be answered by Galena." On 29 September 1970 Galena gave its answer. The plan was defeated, 1,362 to 340.

Ten years have taken some, but not all, of the edge off of the disappointment. "It's funny," Buehler says with a mirthless laugh. "The opposition was fueled primarily by two people who owned buildings that would have been torn down. 'You're destroying our business' they'd say to me. 'You're stealing our property.' I was the big bad outsider. Well, I'm still here but they're gone. They both sold their property. One's moved out to the edge of town. The other never lived in town. Galena's problem is the same as all small towns. They won't commit themselves. They talk all the time about industry, but they're not going to get industry because industry wants cheap labor and there's not much of a labor force here. Tourism should be the industry here. You could take all the downtown away and people would still come because of the natural beauty of the setting. The whole town should be working on making this place so attractive that people would want to come and live here or have a second home here. It could be the loveliest living spot in the whole region. It has the potential, but it's not going to happen if you sit around and say, 'Hey, why doesn't somebody do something?' I thought I was getting along fine. I ran a program for the kids, I got better salaries and pensions for the people who worked in city hall, I was doing things. I had people tell me, 'You'll be remembered forever by this town.' Well, I will be, but not for the reasons they thought."

There Is (Was) a Small Hotel

The DeSoto House Hotel is, by virtue of its size, its location, its history, and its purpose, the solar plexus of Main Street. A large, square, orange brick building, it stands a block or so inside the floodgates and acts as a beacon to tourists and residents alike. When it was built in 1853 it was the largest and most luxurious hotel in the west. Newspapers of the day vied for adjectives with which to describe the elegance of its parlors and reading rooms and the sumptuousness of its velvet carpets and satin draperies. Abraham Lincoln and Stephen A. Douglas spoke from its balcony. Ulysses S. Grant made it the headquarters of his presidential campaign. Jenny Lind sang from its graceful curving staircase.

By the late 1970s its carpets were thin and threadbare; its wallpaper stained; its hall dim if not plunged into darkness by burned-out bulbs; its furniture mismatched and unlovely (a maple student desk and a six-foot carved mahogany headboard); its sheets darned; its mattresses lumpy; its springs noisy; its curtains fiberglass; its fire exits ropes coiled on the floor by the window; and its hot water, hope dashed on a hourly basis. Nevertheless, it was the genuine article in an age of artifice, and it had that raffish charm possessed only by the real. It was also the only hotel in town.

I remember one of my early visits. I was following a whiskey-voiced, caftan-gowned woman who had been summoned from the noisy and lively bar to show me to my room when I noticed a small, dark object clinging to the wall by the grand staircase. Seeing that I had paused, she turned and said, "That's just a bat, honey. I hadn't seen a bat for forty years before I came here, either, but they won't bother you. They've got radar."

It was the sort of place where there was never anyone at the front desk but where two old geezers sat just inside the front door, fly swatters across their knees and chairs tilted back, from dawn until dark; where half the customers at the boisterous bar at any given moment had worked behind it at another; where kids played pinball machines while their parents recovered from traveling with them; where people wandered in from the street to make phone calls and use the bathroom; where messages were left and people met; where you went to find out what was going on and just because you felt like company. It was the general store of everyone's fantasy with the cracker barrel replaced by the bar, and probably more real because of it. The story of the rise and fall of the DeSoto is a story about all that is frustrating and discouraging about small-town life, but it is also a story about resilience, and therefore, hope.

Jim Clayton was a salesman of point-of-purchase advertising materials, working out of Chicago and responsible for the eastern half of the United States, when he saw the advertisement for a hotel for sale. He had no idea where Galena was, but he knew he was sick of traveling, sick of being stacked up over O'Hare for three hours on a Friday night, and sick of spending so much time in New York. He phoned Judy and suggested that they go and take a look at it. They drove to Galena on a gloomy, dirty, slushy Sunday in January, and found the town grim and the hotel grimmer. Nevertheless, the idea was exciting and they couldn't think of any reason not to do it. ("The difference between people who want to change their lives and those who actually do," says Judy in retrospect, "is often simply that the latter ones run into a situation.")

They went back to Arlington Heights, bought a fifteen-cent "For Sale" sign at the local dimestore and stuck it on the lawn in front of their house. They sold it the next day. With the proceeds from the sale, a loan from the bank, and a second mortgage from the owner of the hotel, they put together the $61,000 purchase price and six months later moved in. Jim, who had preceded Judy and the children by a month, had demolished the suite of rooms where their apartment would be and removed most of the rubble, but the new walls were yet to go up. The first night they slept in beds lined up in a row with suitcases at the foot, like an illustration from *Madeline,* and chalk lines to indicate where the walls of their new home would be. When they got up the next morning, they started running the hotel. Judy assumed responsibility for the housework and deskwork and correspondence while Jim was building the apartment and beginning the renovation. Running the hotel was a twenty-four-hour-a-day job; it had never closed its doors for so much as an afternoon in more than a hundred years. Eventually they compromised, putting a lock on the door and a buzzer above it to summon the "night manager"—themselves.

By the time they had acquired the hotel, all vestiges of its former grandeur were buried—the tin ceiling under pink paint and years of filth, the walls under pea-green stucco, and the floor under gray and white linoleum tiles. The lobby furniture was 1940s tubular chrome and vinyl, and a single bare bulb hung over the front desk. They ripped up the tiles and sanded and polished the hardwood floor until it gleamed. They had wallpaper custom-designed to cover the pea-green walls. They replaced the bare bulb with a chandelier and the forties' furniture with a round sofa they'd seen in an engraving of General Grant receiving guests in the lobby. They opened a restaurant that Judy still looks back on with pride, and a bar that quickly became the town meeting place. Nor were their efforts only cosmetic. They gave it a new roof and a new boiler, and cleared the basement of decades of debris.

"We were convinced we could do anything and everything better than anyone else. We were the experts. A lot of times that's all you need—just gall," says Judy. For about five years everything went along nicely, but gradually the hotel began to call for more money than they could afford. "We didn't want to run it without doing things the way they should be done," says Judy, "and we didn't have the resources to do them. We had already spent big money and we were extended as far as we could go. I suppose you could say that we didn't research it carefully enough before getting into it, but you'd be wrong, because we did, very carefully, as is evident from the fact that it supported us nicely for five years. But there's no book you can read that's going to tell you what you're going to run into when you embark on something that big."

They put it up for sale, and after two years finally found a buyer in Orlando Valente, a businessman from Lisle, Illinois. Valente had already purchased the county poor farm on the edge of town, and the county jail, but no one had paid much attention. They did now. Long-term guests were given notice. Out the hotel windows came chunks of plaster, and pieces of marble and sinks and bathtubs. Taped to the entrance was a crayoned notice "Closed for Renovation" on a piece of poster-board, a poignant counterpoint to the blue and gold standard on the corner that declared the hotel an historic site and told of its previous glory. An advertisement in the *Galena Gazette* announced an auction. Everything would go: the armoires, the rocking chairs, the brass cash register, the barroom doors, the beds, the linen, the china—even the lengths of rope that had served as fire exits.

The auction took place on a cold and sunny morning in early December. It was the weekend of the town's annual Christmas Walk, when every storefront is decked out in red velvet and boughs of evergreen, and every storekeeper has a pot of steaming coffee and a plate of homemade cookies just inside the door. The DeSoto had never looked more forlorn. Townspeople and tourists filled the frigid lobby from wall to wall, their breath making cold little puffs in the air. Above them, on the graceful, curving staircase, stood the auctioneer, one boot carelessly placed on the bannister. "Last chance for a memento from the old DeSoto House, folks," he began, and seven hours later, at twilight, it was all over. Who was this man who had bought our hotel, closed it down, and sold the very fixtures off the ceilings?

There is a glancing, Alice in Wonderland quality to conversations with Orlando Valente, to wit:

Q. "How did you happen to come to Galena?"

A. "There are three stages in the evolution of man: hunting, agriculture, and industry. During the hunting stage. . . ."

But Valente is not the Mad Hatter. He suffers from a

simple case of mistaken identity—from the assumption that anyone who buys a seventy-room hotel in an advanced state of deterioration, requiring $1.5 to $2 million to restore must be a businessman/investor with a grand plan. Wrong.

"There comes a time in the hierarchy of human needs when man reaches out for harmony, for a proper surrounding for the development of mind and spirit, for a place where he can look into the mirror and see his soul," he says. The time, for Valente, was the late 1970s; the mirror, Galena. Valente had come to the United States from Italy in 1960 at the age of twenty-one, the oldest of seven children. Within the year, working as a day laborer for the Chicago Brick Company loading bricks into a wheelbarrow, he had brought his entire family over, from his fifty-year-old father to his three-year-old sister. The next year he was drafted. After discharge, he got a job as an electrician at the Burnham Harbor, Indiana plant of Bethlehem Steel, and a few years later went into business for himself as an electrical contractor. He was successful, and the business expanded to include a large retail lighting-fixtures store. Galena may not have been ready for Valente, but Valente was ready for Galena. Not only was it "the proper surrounding for the development of the mind and spirit" but its history was a testament to rugged individualism, and to the rags-to-riches legend which to Valente symbolizes the American character, and, one suspects, his own. He came, he saw, and he bought. First he purchased the poor farm, then the jail, then the hotel. "It was not a good move, economically speaking," he says, "but not all motivations are economic in nature." It is precisely this which troubles the people of the town, who imagine its key structure with its windows forever gaping, its halls forever silent, its doors forever barred. "I can understand their concern," says Valente. "It's their town. But I don't have $1.5 million. It will be very gradual. Rome was not built in a day."

Valente is not greatly loved in Galena, but he has at least one defender: Jim Clayton. "The property was on the market for two years and two months," he says, "and that was time enough for someone to have done something. It was the power structure's default. The trouble is, instead of doing something themselves, they're always looking for that fairy godmother to come and wave a wand and make our community wonderful. One of the earliest potential buyers was a developer who was interested in funding the hotel's rehabilitation through municipal bonds. In order to get institutions interested in buying bonds, you have to show local support. So he went to the banks of Galena. One turned him down flat. The other offered to buy a single $500 bond.

"When anyone knocks Valente, I get up on my hind legs. He's a man who is trying to work against tremendous odds—his own financial limitations and the physical condition of the building. When you renovate a building you want it to last, so you tear it apart to see what's inside. Everytime he tore something apart he found disintegration, so he had to keep tearing.

"How do I feel about Galena now? That it's a backwater. That it's the end of the earth. When I came, I wanted to be involved in everything, and the community wanted me. After I'd been here a month I was elected secretary of the Chamber of Commerce. By the next election I was vice-president, and by the next, president. But then you begin to realize that your efforts don't make any difference, *because no matter how hard you work, nothing changes.* And the reason you can't change things is because you weren't born here. If you're not native-born, your ideas will go awash. The source of the idea is still more important than the crux. You get so frustrated, you just drop out."

I asked Daryl Watson, the administrative assistant to the mayor, if he thought Clayton was right. Watson was born and raised here. He grew up on a farm, received his B.A. from the University of Wisconsin's nearby Platteville campus, and his M.A. and Ph.D. in historical geography from the University of Illinois. He readily agrees with Clayton that Galena is frustratingly slow to change, but his view of what is responsible is quite different.

"As far as who presents an idea being as important as the idea itself—can you name a place or a situation where that isn't the case? *How* you say something counts, too. But that's all normal. Galena isn't any worse than any place else. What is different is that here there's no group that wants to or can work together, and that's what makes change so slow and so difficult. There are the antique shops that open or close as they please; there are the stores that serve the local residents like the furniture stores; and then there are the taverns that won't work with anybody. Then you add the city people who have a still different set of values into the mix, and there is no cohesion and no consensus. But Galena has *never* gotten along with itself. Galena people have *always* fought among themselves like cats and dogs. They're happiest when they're fighting. It is a place of rugged individualists—historically, and to this day. It was a so-called melting pot—Irish manual laborers, German businessmen, you name it—but they didn't even go to the same churches. Even today you have two Catholic churches: Saint Michael's, which is Irish, and Saint Mary's, which is German. They tried to get together a few years ago and gave up after a couple of meetings."

Watson is far more worried about rapacity than inertia. "Tourism is benefiting Galena but it's screwing the hell out of the country," he says. "People visit here and see a house and fall in love with it and restore it, but those same people may go out and without thinking twice about it, put up a shoddy subdivision or sell lots to get rich quick. I wouldn't worry so much if the county had any control, but it doesn't. I'm on the county planning committee and it's basically a plat-approval committee. We get subdivision proposals, and if they meet certain standards we have to approve them. You drive along and you look out and see pastoral countryside, cattle grazing, and a beautiful view, and you hope it will never change. *It already has.* It's been subdivided and is being held for speculation. Its future is housing—or worse—commercial. Jo Daviess County is a wilderness area compared to Chicago, and if you want to save a wilderness area the best way to do it is to limit access, but the reverse is happening here: tourism is attracting people to the area. That's why I say tourism may be good for Galena, but not for the county. Chicago has eight million people and it's only one hundred fifty miles away. Land control is the only answer."

It may be the only answer, but it will be an uphill battle, the likes of which makes Buehler's seem pale by comparison. "There's a strong cultural tradition of private property here," says Watson, "which means anti-zoning. I'm from a farm and I know farmers. They'll tell you they don't want to see it change, but on the other hand no one's going to tell *them* what to do! Then you've got your realtors. They've consistently fought zoning. Their record on historic preservation is terrible. Galena's zoning ordinance wasn't enacted until 1975 and there's *still* no zoning in Jo Daviess County."

If a county zoning ordinance were introduced, I think I know at least one newcomer who would be right there with the rest of the farmers voting against it. I know him pretty well. He would be torn by the choice, because he cares deeply what happens here, but he also cares deeply about the loss of personal freedom to government. He's the man who left Evanston because of building permits and parking meters and "You MUST turn right" signs. But on the other hand, he might surprise me. You never know.

The darkened hotel, the empty hardware, the "For Rent" signs in the store windows, the first faint beginnings of a shopping center out on the highway—all these suggest that Buehler was entitled, were he so inclined, to repeat the words of Hezekiah Gear to the people of Galena a hundred years before: "Gentlemen, you have ruined your town. Grass will grow in the streets."

But there's a movie now, and Donna Basch's bookstore, and the new restaurant, and a new clothing store. The Fulton Brewery, whose windows were boarded and whose roof was collapsing back in 1970 when the referendum was up for a vote, is now a popular shopping mart for tourists, with stalls of antiques and pottery and crafts of all kinds. The Coatesworth Building has risen from the rubble, and provides first-class housing for the elderly. The state is putting a new footbridge across the river, and a new vehicular bridge is planned. And the first new industry in decades—a division of Minneapolis Honeywell—is building a plant at the edge of town that will employ one hundred and fifty people.

We still stand around at parties and talk about What To Do About Galena, and there is still cause for concern. As Watson says, "Galena is stable, but not well." We worry especially about the hotel, whose crayon and cardboard "Closed For Renovation" sign has been replaced by a painted wooden sign that says "CAUTION—DANGEROUS BUILDING—STAY AWAY!" We worry not just because it's part of the town's history and important to the town's economy (after all, you have to have someplace to sleep if you want to have tourists) but because it is part of our *own* history. We slept there the first time we ever came to Galena, and we celebrated there when we bought our houses and we used its rest rooms and showers while we waited to get our own in working order, and we put up our families there when they came to see what on earth we'd gone and done this time.

I don't know what Valente is going to do with it, but I do know that even though he has riled up the whole town, there is a sense in which he belongs here, along with all the other ornery, irreverent, stubborn, anarchic human beings, old and new, who people this place. And if the DeSoto House should end up less than a perfect reconstruction, if it should have, say, a moosehead over the bar or pinball machines in the lobby, well, so be it. That's Galena.

PART THREE

❧ *16* ❧

Celebration

The landscape has begun to wilt and yellow, like flowers left too long in a vase and with the same dispiriting effect. The garden has given its all; the walks each morning and evening yield no more surprises; the year is on the wane. Summer, says a friend, is too much—too much of everything. She's right, and I'm glad to be done with it. Still, I miss anticipation. My forward thrust is thwarted; I am becalmed.

The spiders know; they weave webs as large as dinner plates from zucchini and tomato. Early in the morning when the webs are wet with dew it is a lovely sight: a garden of silvery semaphores. The sunflowers, once so radiant, now hang their heads, a thousand Malacca umbrellas. The corn grows spectral. I would like to grow old like the corn: angular, dramatic, stripped to the spirit. How much more beautiful it is now than it was in its greenness. Each stalk, a dancer; the field, a corps de ballet.

We can walk again, and do. The sweltering heat and swarming mosquitoes of summer are gone. The fields are crisscrossed with the paths of deer. We stuff our pockets with hickory nuts and black walnuts, and breath their pungent scent from our fingertips. This is the season of mushrooms and we fill our baskets with puffballs and chicken mushrooms, a forager's feast. Others, less certain, lie on the table in my study to be examined and compared with descriptions in the book. Are the gills close together or far apart? Decurrent or adnate? Is the stem pillarlike or bulbous? Is the cap scaly, smooth, waxy, or sticky? What color, shape are the spores? The question of edibility is a mere gambit. What is involved here is the passion to know. To know and to name. To fix. To finish. To be without word is as maddening as to hear a melody without the resolving chord.

The maples fade and the oaks rise, a deep muted rose. It is time to pick the corn. There will be five of us today: Dick, three friends from the city, and myself. To pick a field of corn with your own two hands is not a rational act. It is, in fact, tantamount to making your own bricks. For decades corn has been picked by machines whose pointed snouts move between the rows like the teeth of a comb through hair, lopping off the stalk, separating the ear from the stalk, and sending it up a crude, sandbox-style elevator from whence it tumbles into a wagon dragged behind. Actually, even this is old-fashioned; on most farms the picking and shelling operations are done simultaneously by combines that release a blurred stream of golden kernels into waiting hopper cars.

Not here.

I walk between the rows, grab an ear with my left hand, slide my right under its papery husk, grasp the ear inside, twist it back and forth until it is free of the stalk, and then hurl it into the waiting wagon. I have two views as I work: the burnishing hills of Iowa as I grasp and pick; the house and garden as I hurl. I get the sky with each: a great blue bowl, paler at the edges, deeper in the center, visible in its entirety from rim to rim. Sometimes we work five abreast, sometimes three. Finally several voices call for organization. Leaders emerge: "You take this row and I'll take that one," but it's no good—the rows stop and start, appear and disappear. We learn to work together. When my row ends I move far ahead on yours and work back to meet you.

There are stunted ears and twisted ears and ears with only a handful of kernels on the wine-colored cob, but there are also strong, beautiful, perfect ears, and they are in the majority. We did this! We made this corn grow! Our yield will be nothing like our neighbors', but it will be more than our livestock can use. Like everything else we have attempted since we have come here, it is less than perfect, but it is good enough.

As pleased as we are with our success, and as pleasant as it is to pick corn on this gorgeous day, there is trouble afoot. If we don't find a corn-picker at the next auction, Dick says, he's going to leave the rest in the field over the winter. I am alienated as always by the idea of not finishing. It is wrong, it is wasteful, it is sloppy. No, he says, it is not. All he wanted was enough corn to winter over the livestock in the first place, and we already have that. What do I care? I did not plow it, plant it, cultivate it. But to leave the corn in the field . . . ! It is the old, the endless conflict between us, between my linear view of life, and his of life as a tree with an infinite number of branches, all equally fascinating. There is no situation I can conceive of which would have put more stress on us than this farm; it is a miracle we have survived.

At the auction we don't find a corn-picker, but we find a round baler for $200 and a red velvet chair for $1. The baler is the second we have bought in two weeks' time. Its function is to supply spare parts for the first, but upon getting it home we discover that it is in better shape than its predecessor, so we will cannibalize that one instead. I kid Dick about spending two hours of down time for every hour of baling, but he is immune. Its intricacy is what he loves.

"No, no, not off the tree! Off the ground!" He shakes his head in mock despair. Was it not I who complained that I could not walk without crushing apples underfoot? Was it not I who said the place smelled like a vinegar factory?

"But they're *rotten*. They have mushy brown spots, and slugs, and mud on them. We can't use *those*."

"Anything less than half-rotten is okay," he says with the authority of one who has pressed many apples. "That's the whole point."

And so it is. The point of making cider is to use up the bruised, the rotting, the infiltrated, the desiccated, the unlovely. The cider press is like a stockpot: an act of thrift and respect and appreciation. I fill my basket from the ground, fastidious at first, holding each apple by thumb and middle finger as I examine it, debating how much rot is acceptable, then wiping the mud and slugs off in the grass.

But I quickly fall behind. Dick has already filled his basket and poured it into the hopper and the chips of red peel and white apple flesh are already falling into the slatted oak bucket. I hurriedly finish filling my basket, pour its contents into the hopper, and take the other handle. We stand on either side of the press, leaning our weight into the handles as they go down, pulling up as they return. It is pleasant work, rhythmical, with just enough resistance to feel that it *is* work. The sound of the rumbling, rattling metal is satisfying, a kind of instant feedback. When the bucket is full, we slide it forward under the huge iron screw which will press the juice from the apples. The screw is operated by a wheel like a ship's wheel, except that it is set horizontally. I grasp and turn, grasp and turn, until I cannot move it any longer; then I insert a long wooden instrument that looks like a squared-off baseball bat between the handles and let leverage do the rest. All the while the amber liquid is oozing out of the slats of the bucket and running down the wet, dark floor of the press to the hole at the front, where it escapes into the big wooden salad bowl we have put there to catch it, and the bees are doing their kamikazi flights into the froth and drunkenly bumping into everything like boorish party-crashers.

Dick carries the bucket of already-browning apple remains to the barnyard, where the cattle have gathered expectantly by the fence, licking their lips with their huge pink tongues in a parody of a parody. I go into the house for cups for our own tasting. We dip into the bowl and drink. What happens next is astonishing. The sweet-tart flavor of apple cider suffuses from the tongue to the roof of the mouth to the cheeks until every cell of the mouth is reverberating. It goes on and on, like the vibrations of a bell in the air after the tolling has stopped. It is clearly too good a thing to keep to one's self. We decide to have a party. There is no question what kind of party it will be. All parties here are the same: "Bring the children and a dish to pass." Only the excuse and the location change. Our excuse is the cider press. As the days pass, the list of people grows longer and longer. It is a euphoric response to a vision—a vision of a hoedown/square dance/wedding/church supper. The euphoria increases with each invitation rendered: it is going to be *wonderful.*

We grade the road, move the cider press from where it has been from the day that we bought it to where it should have been all that time, pick up the trash of a dozen windy days and the tools of a dozen careless ones. In the house we go for the cobwebs as well as the dust-balls; we clean the top of the refrigerator and under the bathroom sink. It is galvanizing and purifying: a cleansing of the temple in preparation for the feast. Not artifice, after all, this fixing up for company, but honorable ritual.

The day of the party dawns warm and sunny. It is a Sunday—the right kind of day for this kind of party. The house looks as well as a half-finished farmhouse can. Perhaps some day it will be better, perhaps not. It makes no claims, future or present. It is simply where we live. Now the fun begins. We pick up bales of hay from the hayfield and put them in a circle in front of the house, gather the wood for a fire, make tables out of doors and sawhorses and put them on the porch, fill baskets with sheaves of marigolds, put some fiddling music on the stereo. And then, it is happening. The grass is full of people, the kitchen is full of food, the barnyard is full of children, and the air is full of palpable enjoyment. I am done, out of it. It has a momentum of its own now. It is a Methodist dinner, an Elks breakfast. The kitchen is the proverbial groaning board: peach pie, blackberry pie, pecan pie, upside-down cake, chicken, chili, three-bean salad, cornbread, deviled eggs, potato salad, coleslaw, macaroni . . . Tupperware and crockpots and electric frying pans. A gallon of pickles, a bottle of wine.

In the orchard, the word goes from one person to another, "Anything that's less than half-rotten. . . . " A young man I've never seen before races across the barnyard, pulling an old sulky with an ecstatic child in its seat and a dozen others racing after. I introduce two of my guests to each other, and they spend a few moments placing each other in the tribes of Galena ("Isn't your mother . . . ?" "No, that's my aunt . . ."). I listen, bemused, an outsider, but later in the evening find myself saying to a teenaged girl I've never seen before "You must be

Tim White's sister—you look just like him." Kate will hear it someday, too. Does already, in fact. The man in the lumber store tells her "I know where you got that red hair!"

I remember on our first visit to Galena hearing an elderly woman on the street tease two teenage boys about having seen them driving through town, honking their horn in celebration of graduation the night before, and thinking that it was too bad that we had come to this life so late, for our boys would not be here long enough to experience that sort of belonging. But I was wrong. Bea Limback tells Mike that she saw him at band practice and his pivot was wonderful and Cracker tells Bill he saw him going into the pool hall. It is not just that the children of the town are recognized as so-and-so's girl or boy who lives on such-and-such a street, although that is important, but that the children recognize the adults of the community in a similar manner.

Long ago, before we ever thought of moving to the country, I asked Bill how he would change our lives if he could. It was an idle question, a conversational gambit in the spirit of "If you had a million dollars. . . . " He considered it a while and said, "Well, I wish you had more friends"—a strange response from an adolescent, I thought. It seems to me now that he sensed what was missing from our lives before I did. Not friends, per se, but attachments. Life in a small town is like the final overlay on a blueprint: dense with the crosshatchings and parallel lines and shadings and colorings that appear singly on the underlayers. We are joined by a deep and abiding bond: the bond of place. There may be seasons to our affection, but there is no end to our union. As I look at my neighbors (and in a small town we are all neighbors) gathered together in clusters on the grass like the temporary harmonies of notes on a staff, and then out at the misty hills beyond, I think how strange it is that having achieved the solitude of this hilltop, I now prize the human connection.

On the Fourth of July we watched the fireworks here alone. The showers of red and blue and golden light were marvelous from this perspective, but the only sounds I heard were the sounds of frogs and insects. I missed the "Ooooooooh" and "Ahhhhhhhh" of shared pleasure. Perhaps a certain amount of space is necessary for people to want to come together. Perhaps the human spirit, like the eye or ear, can only tolerate so many stimuli before banging closed the shutters and bolting the door. A suburb is like a bead on a necklace. A small town is like the circle a wagon train makes at nightfall on the prairie: warming, protecting, connecting. Like the circle around this fire.

◄§ *17* §►

November

It takes a lifetime to penetrate the symbols of the seasons learned in childhood—to understand, finally, that Christmas is not the heart of winter but only its beginning; that April rarely brings spring; that the brilliance of October is not fall's metaphor but its overture.

It is November now. The trees are bare. There is still color, but it is as weak as an echo, like the light from a star long gone: the dry, straw-color of cornfields, the silvered green of pasture, the dark umber of naked timber and brush spreading from horizon to horizon, as if the land had been consumed by fire. The sky is pale; the sun, cold and distant, as impersonal as a midday moon. The shards of stalk left in the cornfields return the light like bits of metal. The birds are gone now, except for the drab sparrows who steal tufts of insulation from the eaves, and an occasional blue jay or woodpecker. The wind billows and rends the plastic sheeting that covers the wood pile. Eight cords. Already we can see the inroads we have made. Each morning now we must break the thin sheet of ice that covers the surface of the horse trough so that the livestock can drink.

"Is it winter yet, mama?" asks Kate.

No, not yet. I know now that *this* is fall, this reduction

of nature to bare bone and sinew.

The apple trees are bare now, and the earth is hard with frost. In the house, the flies have been replaced by mice, the crickets by fuzzy-wuzzies, and the smell of woodsmoke is always in the air. But the greatest change is the change in scope, and I welcome it with grateful heart. I have had enough of growth and harvest, enough of woods and fields. I long for the interior life as for a day of rain in the midst of summer.

We prepare for winter as for a long trip. Have we forgotten anything? Will we have enough? It dominates our thoughts. The weather, which we used to glimpse through the window like a town on a Greyhound bus, is now a central presence in our lives. We know the hours of sunrise and sunset and precisely where on the horizon to look for each; we know the angle of the sun and which way the wind is blowing. I watch the sky like a mariner. It is my greatest joy—better than the river, better than the valley. Sunrise, sunset, clouds, storm, rainbow—it is an Oriental scroll, endlessly unfurling.

As we prepare for winter I wonder once again at how little is made of the difference between life in warm and cold weather climates when the amount of effort required to live in the latter is so formidable. Water will cease to run, livestock will starve, flesh will freeze—*unless we do something.* Nothing can be taken for granted. Over and over, we begin again. Put away these clothes; take out those. Drain the water, put in antifreeze. Take down the screens, put up the storms. And yet, there are rewards: the lemon-yellow maple, the scorched oak, the burning sumac; the tender green ferns, the purple violets, the rosy columbine.

When Kate wakes up from her nap, we decide to go for a walk in my valley. She races far ahead. It is enough that we do this thing together; no further interaction is necessary. When we reach the valley, we follow the run-off creek. It is not a proper creek, but only a watercourse cut into the earth over the years by the run-off of water from the hills, and it is dry except in the spring and after a heavy rain. But if it is good enough for a beaver and a frog, which I have seen there, it is good enough for me. Today we find the tracks of deer and raccoon frozen into the mud, a reminder that the hunting season is upon us. Kate finds a cache of hickory nuts, and we sit on a rock and exchange them, pretending they are apples and pears and pieces of birthday cake. When the sun drops behind the hill, it is too cold to stay. But before we leave I ask her to be quiet so that we can listen. From far off, there is the knocking of a woodpecker. Then silence. The valley is empty. It is the time of the hunter.

When we return to the house, Ray is at the kitchen table, talking with Dick. He wants to know if Dick is going to trap. The first ads began appearing in the *Galena Gazette* weeks ago—"Hunters and Trappers: The Great Kishwaukee Fur Company will be stopping Saturdays at Clark's Truck Stop at 9:30 A.M."—and now when you go past Clark's or the bowling alley or the car wash or the Farmer's Exchange you see men and boys with raccoons and muskrats and minks spread out in the front of the "rat wagons" and the buyers running their hands down the fur and blowing on it to see if it's prime. Hunting and trapping are as much a part of the seasonal cycle here as putting up storm windows in the suburbs, and there is as little question of ethics involved. Except for us.

We must say yes or no to the men from the city who have hunted deer on this farm for the past twenty years and who want to know if they can do it again this year; to the townspeople who want to hunt coon and already have our neighbors' permission; to the man proferring the bag of freshly caught catfish who is going to be work-

ing his way down the Galena River with his dog and will
therefore go through our property whether or not we
say yes; and finally, we must decide whether we are
going to hunt and trap ourselves. We have already been
out with Ray, without guns, tromping through the
woods and cornfields in the moonlight to see if Herman,
the dog Ed left us, knows how to tree a coon. (He did,
but he also got badly cut-up in a fight with one in the
underbrush.)

The decision on the deer is easily made. They are our
cherished guests (or are we theirs?). At any rate, this
farm, with its thick woods and brushy ravines, will be a
safe place for them. The decision on trapping is more
difficult because it is more abstract: we never see raccoons or muskrat but we do see people like Ray, who
have trapped all their lives, and know them to be decent,
sensible, good men. We suspect, in fact, that they are
infinitely more respectful of nature, and have a more
profound understanding of it, than those who oppose
trapping on the basis of a direct-mail piece or a slick
advertisement. Dick decides he will try it this season,
and see how he feels about it. He will not sell the skins,
though. He already knows how he feels about that: you
use what you kill; otherwise you don't kill. I will be a
spectator for I have no strong feelings one way or the
other. In the last analysis, you choose what you will be
impassioned about: the taking of whales, slum landlords,
strip mining, child abuse, poor schools, the disappear-
ance of saltwater swamps, carcinogens in our foods,
arson, terrorism, the tearing down of historic buildings,
loyalty oaths for judges, and on and on. I am so continu-
ously outraged by the opposition to equal citizenship for
women, and proposals which would deprive me of control over my own reproductive system, that I am drained
of outrage for anything else.

But I am immensely curious—*trapping*, for Lord's
sake, one hundred and fifty miles from the museums and
galleries and high rises of Chicago!—because more than
anything else it reveals what a great distance we have
traveled. I volunteer to take a skunk Dick has trapped to
the Farmer's Exchange, where the Cambridge Hide and
Fur Company stops every Friday and where I learn that
skunk skins are not in great demand, and in no demand
at all when they are on the carcass like this one. ("Skin
one out and you stink for a week," Ray told us.) I hang
around and chat with Larry Moser, the buyer. Moser
tells me that Jo Daviess County probably has the best
production and the best quality of fur in the Midwest,
and that it's because of the hills and bluffs and old quar-
ries and trees, or what game management people call
"habitat." He buys two thousand coon and three thousand muskrats in a week, stopping at small towns like
this throughout northern Illinois and parts of Iowa and
southern Wisconsin. From talking to Ray I know that
the price of raccoon is way up, and I ask Moser why.
"Long hair is in fashion, especially in Europe. Ten years
ago you'd pay five dollars for a coon. Now they're as high
as fifty dollars, even sixty dollars, though they've come
down this season from last." But why, I want to know,
is there such a demand for the fur of living creatures
when we are living in a time of such strong environmen-
tal and ecological concern? *"Because* of that. Because fur's
natural. They want to get back to natural things, and fur
is as natural as you can get." As we talk, men come and
go with their furs. Some are farmers with gun-rests built
into the cabs of their pickups, and cages for their coon
dogs. Others are what Moser calls "schoolboy trappers."
    A farmer lays a single raccoon on the counter in the
cab of Moser's panel truck. Moser examines it.
    Farmer: "How much?"

Moser: "Thirty."

Farmer: "Thirty-five."

Moser: "No."

Farmer: "Yeah, he should be."

Moser: "No, the market's not there. It's dropped off in coon."

Farmer: "Everybody says it's dropped off, but I still see them pay sixty dollars for coon."

Moser: "Then it's an advertisement."

The fellow leaves with his coon, telling Moser "I got twenty-five dollars for one that was *scroungy*-looking compared to this!" and Moser explains to me that a company will pay sixty dollars knowing that the news will travel and the following week they will be swamped with pelts. "They'll buy like hell for one week and pay fantastic money, and then they'll drop off. We're not hot and cold. We're steady." Moser works on commission, so the more money he pays the trapper the more he makes. However, when he gets back to home base, the company looks over the furs he has bought and assigns an average price—say twenty-seven dollars. Then, he says, they'll average the money he's paid out, and if it comes to twenty-eight dollars they'll tell him, "You're paying a little too strong. You'd better slack off." It goes the other way as well. "They'll average them out at thirty dollars and I'll have only paid twenty-eight dollars, and they'll say, 'you're being too tough.' "

What Moser and all fur buyers look for is a coon that's "primed up." "Most trappers don't realize it," he says, "but the quality of a raccoon's fur is determined by the number of daylight hours as well as the weather. They prime up about the same time every year—around November tenth." Specifically, what Moser looks for is at least an inch and preferably an inch and a half of under-wool, thick guard hair (the long black hairs), good color (a blackish blue without a yellow cast), and a white hide. After that, it's a matter of size, which is graded small, medium, large, extra-large, double, and triple.

"There's no exact science to grading," he says. "Different buyers will have different opinions." I tell him the story Ray told me. He caught twenty-one muskrats and went to Fur Buyer A and laid them out in three groups, according to size. The buyer offered him $1 a piece for the skins in the first pile; $4 each for the skins in the second pile; and $7 each for those in the third, for a grand total of $84. He then drove over to Buyer B who offered him $7 a piece across the board, for a total of $147.

Moser says the high price of raccoons has an undesirable side effect: there are a lot of hunters and trappers who don't know what they're doing. I already knew. Michael came home from high school (which automatically gives the Friday of the deer-hunting season off to any student with a license) with the story of the kid who had shot off the front legs of a deer and didn't have another shell to finish him off. A neighbor with a herd of Holsteins—milk herds are supposed to be kept calm —had a stampede on her hands because of hunters. She also had a vendetta on her front lawn. She picks and chooses whom she will allow to hunt on her property. Some men she said no to shot the windshield and tires of the car of those she said yes to. Fences are torn and cattle get out (and sometimes get shot). And then there are the fellows who do their hunting with a blinding light from the comfortable seat of a warm car. Moser has his own definitions of a good hunter and a bad hunter. "A bad hunter is one that would shoot a female coon and her three kits down out of the tree when the four of them together wouldn't be worth twenty-five dollars. A good hunter knows that if there's four coon up a tree, it's a mother and three little ones, and he'll leave them alone."

Moser trapped with his father when he was a kid. "We trapped strictly for mink and muskrat. Even back then mink was twenty-five dollars, which was probably more than the thirty-five dollars we pay now. Coon were only a dollar then. We'd get mad when we'd find one in the trap because it ruined the mink set. And we used to think of a fox as just a mangy old varment." Now the red fox, due to mange and loss of habitat, can bring as high as eighty dollars. "What people fail to realize is that the incentive to retain habitat comes directly from the money that the guy who owns the habitat gets from his fur population," Moser says confidently. "If it weren't for sportsmen and trappers, all the habitat would be bulldozed in and paved with cement."

One's feelings about trapping aside, he's probably right.

Those who should certainly know better—farmers— have already destroyed thousands of acres of habitat by plowing and planting fencerows in order to get the last half-acre of corn possible from the land. As a result, they have driven the red fox from the state, and put a lot of other creatures in jeopardy. There are endangered species in Illinois, as well as Africa. Can developers be trusted to look farther ahead?

Ed Freeman is known locally simply as "the game warden." In fact, he is supervisor of game management for five northern Illinois counties. "Illinois' first deer season in the twentieth century was in 1957," he says. "Deer used to be native to the state, but the encroachment of man on their habitat, and unrestricted hunting, virtually wiped them out. I came here in 1952, and I was probably here two or three years before I ever even saw a deer. They got a start back through live trapping. They were released throughout the state, and they prospered. During that first hunting season in 1957 there were 137 deer killed. It climbed steadily until it reached a plateau of 700 to 800, which is where it is today."

According to Freeman, "game management" became popular immediately after World War II. "A lot of the servicemen went to game management schools and they came back aware that if we were going to have a continuous abundance of game in the states, or any semblance of game for that matter, they had to know how to *manage* game. A wild animal is just like a human being—it has to have something to eat and a place to live in order to survive. It's normal for a healthy doe to have twins, and triplets are not uncommon, so if there's not too much stress during the winter it doesn't take long for the population to build up pretty quick."

Something to eat and a place to live. Jo Daviess County is a Virginia white-tailed deer's paradise. Not only are there large tracts of timber, plus plenty of "edge"—the place where forest and cropland meet and which deer delight in—but city people who buy acreage here don't generally plow up what they have come to enjoy, tending to preserve habitat and offer refuge. As far as food goes, the local joke is that our venison is corn-fed. Freeman says it's no joke. "If a field is picked, there's always corn in that field that the farmer misses, and if it's not picked, all the deer has to do is help himself. Some farmers will yell if they lose just a few kernels. Others won't mind if the deer take a couple of acres for the pleasure of seeing them. But we had a case last year where a farmer had a hundred deer coming to his corn crib. He was pretty unhappy about it. Food's no problem, unless there's a deep snow for a long period. They won't travel in deep snow. They'll bunch up and stay in one place and eat themselves out of house and home. They'll starve to death and maybe over the next hill is food. Why? A one hundred fifty- or two hundred-pound deer will break through the snow where a thirty-five- or forty-pound dog won't. The dog will chase the deer in deep snow until it catches him, and then it'll just tear at his flanks until he's not going to survive. It's hard to convince a local farmer that Rover over there, lying in front of the fireplace, just killed a deer, but I've seen them do it."

"Fortunately for game management purposes, we have an any-animal deer season in Illinois. Any deer in the woods is legal game. In places where they have the buck-only season, it's due to tradition, and tradition is nothing more than your average hunter who doesn't have all his facts together going to his local politician and raising hell. Everyone is an expert in game management—the guy sitting in the bar in the city drinking his beer and the guys sitting around the campfire."

Each county in the state has a license quota. For Jo Daviess, the number is twenty-three hundred. After the kill, each hunter must go to a check station where a count is kept and weight and blood samples are taken. "A deer is like a farm crop," Freeman says, echoing the sentiment of countryside. "There is a surplus to be harvested." Nevertheless, "It's kinda hard to eat deer," says a friend of mine. "I think I still have some in the freezer from three years ago." Her husband allows friends from the city to hunt on their land, and talks about doing some hunting himself, but never quite gets around to it. The other day, he came across a buck and a doe grazing. "I wish I'd had a gun," he said. "It would have been like hitting the broad side of a barn." But then he turned to his wife and added, "I should have honked or done something to scare them so they won't be so trusting."

I believe what Freeman and Moser say. I believe that here, and everywhere, we are so far from wilderness conditions that the laws of the wild, or allowing nature to take its course, won't do the job anymore, and that if we are going to have wildlife for the future, it is people like Ray Leners and Larry Moser and Ed Freeman who will be responsible.

But the farm is still going to be a safe place for deer.

⊸ぅ *18* ⊱

Children

Michael drops his books on the kitchen table and hangs over the shelves of the refrigerator as if they were a delicatessen. He has walked the three miles from school, although the school bus would have saved him two of them, because he likes to do it.

"So? What are we going to do today?" The question is not querulous or martyred. It's just a question, and I no longer gird myself for confrontation.

"Well, you could split wood."

"No, I think I'll work on the road. There's a place at the bottom that's still pretty bad." He has worked on the road after school every day this week. He knows what needs to be done, and I respect his priorities.

School was not easy at first. He is a senior, and shy, and there was not that embracing of strangers I had naively expected from a small school. Here, there are four hundred students; in Evanston there were four thousand. My heart sank when he told me he ate his lunch alone every day. But week by week it's gotten better, and now the ringing of the telephone and the rumble of the unfettered muffler and the roar of the motorcycle is again heard in our land.

When we announced to the family and friends that we

were moving to the country, the first question was always, "How do the kids feel about it?" It seemed a normal response at the time; indeed, it was the first question I had asked myself. After all, we didn't have to move, and moving is generally regarded as tough on kids, especially kids in their last two years of high school. It was our dream. Weren't we being rudely indifferent to their needs and wishes? Why didn't we wait another two years until they would both be out of high school? The answer is that they were a part of that dream. When I thought of living in the country, I thought not of Dick and myself walking alone together on golden summer days, but of all of us together, around a fire, on cold winter nights. It was a dream not of an adventure, but of a *life*.

What doubts I felt at the beginning were assuaged in part by the kids' reactions, or lack thereof. There were no storms of protest, no slammed doors, no outrage, no depression. It was just something that was going to happen. As weekends on the farm became a regular part of our lives, I quickly began to feel that not only were we *not* doing something terrible *to* them, but that we were doing something wonderful *for* them, that we were giving them something rare and special that they would have for the rest of their lives. I still do.

From the beginning, the farm gave scope to Michael's fundamental nature. From preschool days his happiest moments have been spent tinkering—taking apart, rebuilding, inventing. Here was something ready and waiting to be made over: the biggest junkyard in the world. He viewed the ancient tractors, the 1922 outboard motor, the barns and sheds full of tools and parts, with a connoisseur's eye. A steep hill, a motor, and a pulley were instantly perceived as the raw material for a ski slope. An impenetrable thicket at the river's edge was clearly meant to be a dock. By the end of that first winter he knew the farm better than we did. I believe he does still. He never said, "Oh, wow!" Kids don't. But he would disappear for hours on crosscountry skis. He would get up and build the first fire of the morning and tell Dick with relish what a poor job he'd done building it the night before. And he said, until we thought we'd throttle him, "If you ask *me*, here's what *I* think we should do. . . . " The fact is, his ideas were as good as anyone's. We were learning together.

For Bill, life on the farm was utterly the wrong ambience for the persona he was establishing, which was built on city cool. He was a musical sophisticate, a *Dungeons and Dragons* player, a reader. Unlike Michael, who was a loner, Bill had left behind a large number of friends. But there is a certain cachet to exile. When I was Bill's age, I used to spend the summers on my grandparents' farm. I loved the working windmill creaking behind the house, the kittens clustered around the back door waiting for their share of the night's milking, and the modest assortment of cows and pigs and chickens that testified that this was a *real* farm. I hated being told to get my nose out of that book and get out and get some fresh air for heaven's sakes, and I would skulk around the yard until I could slip unnoticed back to my attic bedroom with its copy of *Forever Amber* under the pillow. But it was the best of both worlds: the inner life enhanced by its disparity with the outer, and vice versa. A delicious exile. I think it is much the same for Bill.

When Bill was at Evanston Township High School, he was suspended twice for possession of marijuana—the second time for rolling a joint in the cafeteria at noon hour, in full view of a couple of hundred students and faculty. We could have opened up a head shop with the paraphernalia in his room: papers, rolling machines, roach holders, pipes, air fresheners, incense, books. It was the books that really bothered me. The paraphernalia was normal experimentation. The books suggested a budding ideology. No evidence of experimentation was necessary, anyway: the falling marks, the red-rimmed eyes, the sleeping at odd times and disorientation when awakened told the story. Though he tested in the top percentile, his report cards were filled with C's and D's and finally an F. Here on the farm, marijuana grows wild, as ubiquitous and obvious as gooseberries. He undoubtedly uses it on occasion, but I haven't seen red-rimmed eyes or encountered midday sleeping since we moved here. He goes to bed at a reasonable hour, gets up when called, and is a fairly pleasant fellow across the breakfast table. He now gets A's, B's, and C's. He says the courses are easier and that there is nothing else to do, but I think the answer lies elsewhere. Perhaps when you are fourteen or fifteen or sixteen or seventeen and trying to establish your identity, four thousand people constitute just too big a puddle. There are, of course, other ways to be noticed, but many of them demand that you be a competitor, which requires having a reasonably strong identity in the first place.

In Evanston the kids had numbers. Here in Galena they have nicknames. Everyone gets one. Bill is "Volcano." Michael is "Fuji." It doesn't mean anything. It's just the name of a photographic-equipment manufacturer that's emblazoned across a T-shirt he wears. But it is his alone. He is part of the tribe.

On Halloween the entire town gets in costume for a parade down Main Street at night. There are fathers dressed in capes and tights and boxing shorts carrying daughters dressed as Raggedy Ann. There are mothers in black suits and fedoras and black stockings, carrying fake tommy-guns, accompanied by fierce-looking nine-year-old sons, chomping on cigars. There are humpty-dumpties, pioneer women, little bo-peeps, Civil War soldiers, sunflowers, lady godivas, red riding hoods, horses, floats, and three bands. There is, in fact, scarcely anyone left on the curb to watch. We went, we marched, and we yelled—for Michael on his unicycle, playing the tuba; for the Lutheran minister's two-year-old dressed as a crusader and for the dentist dressed as a conehead, and then we came home. In the light of the car headlights we saw on our new cedar siding two words, written in careful shaving-cream script: *"Fuji." "Volcano."* There was no toilet paper around the tree branches and no egg on the walls and the open doors had not been entered and the pristine expanse of picture window had not been touched, for this was not vandalism. It was hello.

For Kate, the farm has meant a freedom that I could no more have envisioned than she. When we moved here, she had just turned three and her world had just expanded from the confines of the backyard to the sidewalk in front. Today she roams freely, the only limits those she sets for herself. The apple orchard, the barn, the grainery, the chicken coop, the nearby pasture—all are hers. She chases butterflies and chickens and strokes caterpillars to see their backs arch and their bright yellow antennae shoot out. She picks bouquets of wild flowers and baskets of berries. She helps herself to mint and radishes. She climbs the scaffolding on the south side of the house and makes of it a jungle gym. Her swimming pool is a horse trough and her sandbox, the stall full of sunflower seeds. She collects eggs with trepidation and faces heifers fearlessly. And three days a week, for two hours each day, she goes to nursery school in Hazel Green, a twenty-minute drive each way. She has never taken a backward look. Perhaps too much is made of the trauma of moving. After all, a loving family is a moveable feast.

I have no illusions about the next few years. It will be lonely for her when the boys leave for college, and difficult for me because of it. A friend on a farm thinks her ten-year-old son suffers from lack of companionship, even though he has two sisters only a few years younger. But nothing is perfect.

Kate's world is unbelievably rich, not just in the intimate acquaintance with her natural surroundings, but with people. To the same extent that our life here has put us in constant congress with all different types of people, so has her own. She lives in a world where both sexes and all ages are present. Tonight I asked her what she was going to be when she grew up—a carpenter like Jan? An electrician like John Bookless? Would she have a bookstore like Donna Basch? Be an auctioneer like John Balbach? Would she be a farmer like Mr. Dempsey? No, she said. She was going to be "everything." It's not a bad goal.

It is as natural to defend one's choice of territory as to defend territory itself, particularly as regards one's children, and it is conceivable that what I feel when I look out at Michael on the tractor, or at Bill stretched out on the hay wagon, dreamily scratching the goats under the ears, or at Harry splitting wood, or at Kate racing confidently across the vast landscape on four-year-old legs, is nothing more than that. But I think not. The feeling that there is a natural affinity between children and the country, between children and nature, is so universal that it suggests intuitive human wisdom. There is not a parent in the world who does not feel it, even while being pleased and proud that their children are city smart.

Dick is an emphatic believer in children contributing their labor to the family unit, though he recalls with groans and rolling eyes the list of jobs his father left for him when he was a child, and with humor his own attempts at procrastination and evasion. He considers the running battle between generations on this issue a normal part of family living. I, too, believe that children should contribute to the family welfare, and on an almost one-to-one basis as they grow older, but always an idealist, I think they ought to do it willingly because it is clearly the right thing to do. As a result, I am often depressed and frequently avoid the issue entirely, preferring to do the work myself and escape confrontations.

In Evanston the boys helped with the standard household tasks such as cleaning up the kitchen, taking out the garbage, and lending a hand with the once-a-week cleaning. They did the seasonal jobs like cutting the grass and shoveling the snow. And occasionally they were asked to help with major projects like cleaning out the basement or the garage. But beyond that Dick and I were often hard-pressed to find some meaningful work for them to do, and I believe they knew this and responded as anyone does to make-work—with deep resentment and disgust. At best their attitude was patronizing—a conciliatory gesture toward slightly aberrant but generally fair parents. At worst they were hostile.

Here, they are called upon constantly: to mend a fence, to fell a tree, to repair a wagon, to roof an outbuilding. A fence in disrepair means time spent tracking down errant cows; if trees are not cut, we will not have enough firewood to keep warm this winter. The wagon is needed for hauling. The building will rot if the roof is not fixed. It is important work and they know it, but beyond its obvious value, and thus their own value in performing it, there is the additional pleasure of mastery. The satisfaction of competency is greatly underrated. They still resent the indoor stuff—the dishes, the cleaning up—as I do, as we all do, but there is less resentment toward *us* when they have to do it, and I believe it's because we are all leading the same life.

Parenting is largely a one-way street these days, and the returns received largely those provided by a protégé to a patron: a good performance, a pleasing presence. In the country, there is a fairer exchange, and perhaps less guilt on the part of the young and a better relationship because of it. Children with real work to do become responsible members of the community earlier, and are more pleasant to be around. A few nights ago a friend whose garden had been ravaged by the raccoons asked a high-school senior, a farm boy who raises sweet corn, how to keep the coons out of the corn.

You simply get up a couple of times during the night and run the dogs through the corn, he said.

Get up in the middle of the night?

Well sure. How else were you going to keep the coons out of the corn?

I recently discovered a journal I kept when we lived in Evanston and were thinking of moving to the country. It said: "Why the country? To recapture a lost feeling of family-ness before we are a family no more. Dick works, I work, Michael builds bicycles in the basement, Bill listens to his stereo in his room. We have lost the connection." Dick still works, as do I, and the boys still have private lives of their own as well as that which they share with us, but there is a unity to our lives, and a sharing, which was never there before. It is made up of a hundred tiny strands—of watching lightning streak across the sky together and feeling the thunder shake the house and knowing without knowing it that we depend on each other; of sharing the tasks of feeding the animals and keeping the fire and caring for the road; of everyone knowing what the tractor hitch looks like and having an idea of where he last saw it; and of all having made some dumb mistakes. But it is not just that we have shared a thousand common experiences since coming here, but that *we share a common environment.*

A few weeks ago a neighbor called to say she was having a party for a newcomer. Come around five and bring something to cook on the grill and a dish to share. The children? Well, of course! Cars filled the barnyard. The dogs of three families rushed out to greet each new arrival. Kids raced across the lawn, tumbled each other out of hammocks, tossed a football, whispered, giggled, counted to twenty against tree trunks, stole cookies from the buffet and asked parents where sweaters were and when they were going to eat. Parents did what parents do—drank and talked and ate and laughed. As it grew dark and chilly, the younger ones found shoulders to lean against or played chopsticks on the old upright piano, and the teenagers stood on the periphery, listening and watching. Not much interchange, no. Neither is there much interchange between the branches of a tree. It was a magical evening and the magic of it was not that we who were assembled shared a moment's sense of community, but that the moment was part of a continuum. Our daily lives would bring us back to one another again and again.

Long ago I asked Christopher Hirsheimer why she and Jim had left San Francisco. Surely it was more than the cost of living that had sent them from one of the great cities of the world to a little town in the Midwest. Life in San Francisco was so . . . *anxious,* she said. Everyone was "into" something—EST, Esalen, affairs, drugs. Everyone was so busy *looking,* searching, that they never just *lived.*

"I have a theory about it," she continued. "You know

what happens when a hundred rats are put into a maze designed for twenty-five? They become frantic and disoriented. I think the same thing happens to people when there isn't enough space. They're driven to further and further extremes to differentiate themselves, to stand out from the crowd."

A few years ago my best friend and her husband decided to move from the small village where they had lived since their children's preschool days to a large town of famous name. She loved the village they were leaving; the kids loved it; her husband loved it. They lived a half-block from a river chock full of boats; the rigging could be heard clanking against the masts from the kitchen window. The kids had their own boat, a battered dinghy, and used it to explore the beaches and coves and offshore islands. Her husband walked to the train station. Sometimes they would meet him there with a picnic all packed, ready to eat on the beach. She hated change. Moving held as much dread for her as changing jobs might for others. Why, then?

The schools. The kids were very bright. The schools in the famous town were better. Better courses, better teachers, a better preparation for college. The idea of a family wrenching itself from a life it savored and valued and knew was good, for the advantages of a superior system of formal education is disturbing, I think, and what is disturbing about it is the idea that school, that big brick box that anywhere and at any age segregates one from life, is more important than life itself. It is not so far from the search for the right school to the kind of searching that Christopher was talking about, or what another friend calls "looking for the peanut."

In our town, people look for morels each spring, that mysterious, hard-to-find mushroom whose crenelated surface makes it look like a small pear-shaped brain, and whose taste is as rare as truffles. The morel mystique drives virtually every man, woman, and child into the woods.

"Under a dead elm . . ."

"on a south-facing slope . . ."

"where apple orchards used to be . . ."

"not under dead elms, only dying ones . . ."

"after a rain . . ."

"after several hot, sunny days . . ."

"when the apple trees are in blossom . . ."

"when oak leaves are as big as squirrels' ears. . . ."

So I went into the woods and kept my eyes to the ground. After a week of searching daily, I found two morels, but I missed much more. I missed the dozens of discoveries that had made my previous walks through the woods moments of grace and wonder—the bluebird, the sudden sight of a V-wake made by a beaver's tail, the flash of a deer, the scream of a hawk. Who knows what else?

I hope by living here the children will take with them the knowledge that the world is full of peanuts, peanuts for every man's taste, and that one man's peanut may be another man's poison. Dick has a poster he likes with a quotation from e. e. cummings: "To be nobody but yourself in a world which is doing its best night and day to make you like everybody else means to fight the hardest battle any human being can fight and never stop fighting." I never liked it. It seemed arrogant in its paranoia. Who, I used to think, is this "world?" Isn't it just a collection of other people just like you who are fighting the same battle? But if there is no "they," the forces for uniformity are nevertheless undeniable, and they breed a counterforce, the radical swings of styles and mores, and the sometimes violent struggles for identity, that is just as powerful and pervasive. It is this, among other things, that is responsible for the movement from cities and suburbs back to small towns and rural areas. How very strange that the small town, for generations the symbol of the pressure to conform, should today become a symbol of the freedom to live as one will.

⊲ 19 ⊳

The Difference It Makes

There are two things in particular that puzzle friends in the city and suburbs about the life we have chosen. They are usually expressed as "But you work so hard!" and "What do you do?", meaning without movies, restaurants, bookstores, shops, plays, museums, etcetera. I am always amused that the relationship between the two goes unnoticed.

The urban/suburban society is as much a society of consumption today as when Thorstein Veblen wrote *Theory of the Leisure Class.* You can't help it. When I return to the city—and I have spent most of my life in the city—I am overcome with acquisitiveness. I want clothes, cosmetics, furniture, luggage, lamps, art, books, tickets. I want, I want, I want. I am overwhelmed with avarice.

While it may challenge credibility, it is a fact that I rarely want anything in the country. It is, of course, partly a matter of exposure. They don't have all those wonderful things in the country; when I come to the city and see them, I am filled with desire. And it works in reverse. When you live in the city you are certainly not as overcome with cupidity as the visitor; you develop a degree of immunity. But not much.

The difference is there and it is real. The purpose, the raison d'être, of a city is commerce. It is reflected from every wall and window, from every bumper and bus card. The purpose of a small town is a place to live. It is a matter of emphasis, of course, but it is an emphasis that colors daily life.

What do you do when the blandishments of commerce are not a dominant part of your daily life? *What do you do? You work so hard.* As John Bookless says, "People come out here and say 'where's the action?' They don't understand when I say, 'Oh, I cut a little wood.'" Or plow a field. Or plant a hundred spring bulbs. Or open a business. Or restore a house. Or can fifty quarts of tomato sauce. It would be ridiculous to suggest that the acquisitive spirit is absent from small towns or that the work ethic is not alive and well in the city, but in the main I believe that in the country the first response to that eternal question, "What shall we do?" is likely to be some form of work, and in the urban setting, some form of consumption, or to put it another way, some form of doing versus some form of getting.

The differences between the urban culture and the country culture are many and deep, so deep that two people who have spent their lives in an urban environment, no matter what else divides them, are likely to feel more comfortable with each other initially than a city person and a farmer. Here are some of the differences:

People who live in cities, like the *Sesame Street* generation, have been primed by their life experiences to expect the new and different, and to a certain extent to look forward to it. Country people, on the other hand, look for and enjoy the familiar and repetitive—the peonies blooming on Memorial Day, the tiger lilies on the

Fourth of July, bringing in the cattle the day after Thanksgiving. The result is that city people tend to be more responsive to novelties or trends than country people and those in the country, in turn, tend to be cycle-oriented and conservative.

Life in the city is lived largely unaware of what is going on, day by day, in the natural world. In a sense, the natural world is a foreign environment that you pass through as you go back and forth between home and office. In the country, the natural world is the primary environment, a presence that surrounds and colors everything that takes place, like the lighting upon a stage play.

City life puts a high premium upon time. In the country, time is not even thought of as a resource. Time is a well-stocked cupboard: there is plenty, enough for all, and more where that came from. Sit down! Enjoy!

The city encourages the development of a persona, perhaps because there are so many people that it becomes imperative to define ourselves clearly in order to be noticed. The country inhibits it, perhaps because we all know each other too well. In the country, my identity blurs and fades: I am a small figure in a large canvas by Rousseau; in the city, I zoom into the foreground.

The city person lives among strangers; the country person among friends.

There is an entire group of human beings in the city that has no counterparts in the country. I will call them neuters. They are: bank tellers, waitresses, bus drivers, cleaners, taxi drivers, policemen, bartenders, receptionists, museum attendants, ladies' room attendants, and salespersons. Certain individuals within these groups are not neuters, of course, for neuters are not born, but made. You neuter a person when you do not look into his eyes, when you do not speak, and when you go on talking to the person you are with when you enter his presence. It works both ways, of course. Neuters tend to give their neuterdom to you, like the chicken-pox. I am always embarrassed when friends from the city go shopping with me in Galena, for they inevitably behave as if the salesperson isn't there, whereas to me, and more importantly, to her, she's there, her name is Marie, and our kids go to school together.

There are other differences. Says Christopher Hirsheimer: "In the city, you can fool yourself. All you have to do is go to the right place in the right dress and you think 'Aren't I *won*derful sitting in this *won*derful place in this *won*derful dress looking absolutely *won*derful!' But why are you so wonderful? Because you picked that place and bought that dress? What did *you* contribute? You didn't even pick it out—they *sold* it to you. Here, you face each other without supporting backgrounds. There's nowhere to pose and no one's impressed with what you're wearing. It's *you*. And you're going to see the same people day after day for years."

Yes, you are, and it means, as Kathy Webster remembers discovering when she started to honk the horn at someone making a left turn from a right-hand lane, "I can't do that! It might be the checkout lady at the grocery store! It could be the lady at the doctor's office! It could be the man who changes my Culligan water tank! I'll get a reputation!" But relinquishing anonymity—what a strange notion, when you stop to think about it!—is a small price to pay for trust and intimacy.

My grandmother, whose farm I used to visit, used to use a wonderful old-fashioned word that I never hear anymore. *Self-important.* In its place we have "egocentric" and "self-absorbed." While they are more elegant, they lack the punch of Grandma's appraisal. To be self-important was to be shamefully out-of-step, to be suffering from a kind of moral gaseousness. It's hard to remember a time when self-importance was not a virtue but a vice. Living here has given it back.

I heard a waitress at a local restaurant make a mildly unkind remark about one of her friends, and then, instantly chagrined, say, "But I guess I shouldn't talk—I'm that way sometimes, too." I was struck by the incident because implicit in her self-correction was the desire to be a kinder, more morally perfect human being. We seek to perfect many aspects of ourselves these days, from our backhand to our sexual skills, but charity is not notable among them.

It is harder to be self-important in a small town. The impulse to honk, to sigh vocally, to seek special favors, to lose one's temper, to castigate the inefficient and ignorant—all are curbed, at least for the moment, by the lack of anonymity. It doesn't make you a better person, but the moment is an important one, for the suspended judgment paves the way for a more informed, seasoned, and potentially generous one. That doesn't mean that you walk around watching your p's and q's. Something rather more felicitous happens: you begin to realize how pleasant and soothing the rituals of courtesy are, and how rich the rewards of tolerance, which is ultimately a matter of patience. Figuring people out, "placing" them in such a way that they stay put, always a tantalizing game, is now a game without end: a piece here, a piece there, but never finished. What looks like a bit of the border turns out to be a piece of the sky, and everyone knows how long that takes to fill in.

You might think that when you move from the city to the country you would be giving up the pleasure of knowing many kinds of people and would be settling for a more homogenous society. I suppose that may be true in some small towns, but it has not been our experience. I suppose it all depends on what you mean by "many kinds of people." The urban/suburban culture tends to define people by what they do for a living. It's true that I haven't met any physicists or musicians or manufacturers lately, but I've met a plumber whose hobby is doing spins and rolls and cuban eights in a 1946 aircraft he rebuilt in his garage, a gas-station manager whose hobby is catching rattlesnakes alive (last year he caught fifty-seven), and a department-store buyer who cans eighteen hundred quarts of produce for the sheer pleasure of it.

But that's not the point. The point is that when you stop neutering people, when you stop scanning them and discarding the ones whose sensibilities don't match yours, when you admit to consciousness the possibility that you might have something in common after all (or better still, something to learn from one another)—all behavior which is encouraged by the intimacy and permanency of small-town life—it's amazing what diversity you find.

Some people genuinely love the places where they live, and every day of their life is enhanced by being there. For others, it's a matter of indifference or a simple fact of life: you were born there so you stay, or there's a job there so you go. For still others, it's a compromise, requiring fortitude but rewarding in the trade-offs received. And finally, for an ever-growing number of people all across the country, it's an important choice—a choice that takes precedence over what kind of work they will do and how much money they can make at it.

There are signs that people are becoming disenchanted with the price of success, which is often a life which separates living partners, parents from children, one generation from another, home from work, home and work from the natural world, one's present from one's past, and which ultimately fragments the self. Suddenly, what you do for a living is less interesting to other people than what you do when you aren't working. Suddenly, everyone knows someone who's passed up a promotion or a transfer, or who's opted for early retirement or who's changed careers in order to spend more time with his family or in just plain living. Suddenly, people have stopped just talking about "leaving the rat race" and are finding ways to do it. A recent study of men in the twenty to thirty age-group showed that the highest priority was no longer success or power or money, but "love" or "a good family life."

The quest for the good life has led to the country for many. "Back to basics," the cachet that pretends to both describe the phenomenon and explain it, is attractively terse but wrong, since it fails to convey the eclecticism involved. I have met no people while living in the country who have raised all their own food or made their own fuel. The people I know have said, "We choose this, and this . . . but not that, or that"—the thoughtful choices necessary if we are to survive our own technology.

The move to the country is in part the yearning for a simpler life, a more natural life, and a life less centered on consumption, but the nostalgia for these pieces of our past masks a much deeper yearning which has nothing to do with nostalgia. It is the yearning for a *unified* life, for the binding center that cannot be found in self alone, for a single, integrated network where one can work, play, and love. *That* is the simplicity sought in dreams of a simple life, and that is the simplicity that can still be found in smaller communities. It is not that we yearn to be alone, but that we yearn to be together in peace and harmony and simplicity, and in a way that nourishes both freedom and attachment, both independence and interdependence. We yearn to belong to something that is not our own creation, like the network structure of urban life or the closed system of the self-sufficient farm, but that exists outside of ourselves and that has a past. A family is not enough. A farm is not enough. A network is not enough. It takes a community. A community is people who remember it the way it used to be. It's having your days punctuated by chance encounters with people you know. It's being concerned when you hear the fire engine even when you're at home. It's recognizing the butcher without his apron and the bank teller when she's not framed by the teller's cage. It's never wondering if storekeepers think you're a shoplifter and never being asked to produce your driver's license. It's a swimming hole, a haunted house, a Halloween Parade, and a nickname. It's being told, "I know where you got that red hair" and being asked, "Aren't you Michael's mother?"

Certainly some city neighborhoods and suburbs *are* communities in the true meaning of the word, but they are rare, because a feeling of community depends on trust and intimacy, which require for their development a more continuous relationship with one another and with place than is characteristic of metropolitan living today.

While in population and outward appearance suburbs may resemble small towns, in tone they bear a much stronger resemblance to cities. They have the same anonymous and highly mobile population, are characterized by the same neutral and impersonal encounters, are plagued by the same fears of theft, mugging, and rape, and experience perhaps even more acutely than city-dwellers the feeling that life has no center.

One lives here, works there, shops somewhere else. The pharmacist commutes to the drugstore from three suburbs distant; the shoe-store manager lives in the city; the bookstore is a branch; the restaurant is a franchise;

a consultant from the West Coast has built the shopping center; the city manager has just arrived from a university a half-continent away. Faces and places swirl and disappear. What happened to that cute little restaurant . . . the woman who gave such good haircuts . . . the man who ran the corner newsstand? The big green house down the street is up for sale again . . . and did you hear that the Johnsons have been transferred to L.A.?

This is not to suggest that small towns and rural areas are isolated from change. They are changing right now as a result of the many people who suddenly want to live in them. A working, 240-acre farm becomes three 80-acre retirement farms. The feed store, lacking business, closes its doors and moves down the road to the next town. The local variety store feels pressure from the discount stores of the nearest metropolitan area. The downtown is endangered by the ubiquitous shopping center. But because a small town is almost by definition surrounded by a rural area, the changes are slower, more a matter of evolution than contagion, of cautious choice than trendy conformity. Because a small town has a past and people who remember it and treasure it, it is slower to welcome the future with open arms. Small towns also have an ethic of independence. An elegant native of Galena, reminiscing about the failure of the Buehler referendum, pursed her lips in disapproval and said with a sigh, "Galena's spirit can be summed up in eight words: 'Nobody's going to tell me what to do!' "

I'm not sure that's such a bad philosophy. It seems to me a truculent expression of something we're a little short of these days: self-reliance. When you're out of practice in the arts of both self-reliance and self-sufficiency, it's easy to confuse the two. Self-reliance means being confident of one's own judgment and abilities. Self-sufficiency means getting along without help, and indeed, one of its dictionary definitions is "having too much confidence in one's own abilities and powers."

I aspire toward self-reliance, but I want no truck with self-sufficiency. Living here, on a farm, at the edge of a small town, I have learned, finally, that I need people, need the chance encounters with familiar others, need the rituals of courtesy, need the welcoming nod from the stranger, need a center beyond self. Life is too complicated to deal with alone, and the pleasure of sharing too great to forego.

There is something about those chance encounters that is deeply satisfying. It is not a substitute for the deeper encounters of friendship, nor an evasion of them but a unique pleasure unto itself. Perhaps it is the same pleasure as that which the infant obtains from the game of peek-a-boo: the realization that there is a continuity outside one's self. Perhaps it is a reminder that there is still territory, still more depth to be explored; that when you count your friends and write your Christmas cards you haven't reached the end; potential abounds. It is, in fact, one of the curiosities of living here that the town, instead of becoming smaller with familiarity, becomes larger. Is it because we are still fairly new and much preoccupied with our own lives? Will we exhaust it after a few years? I think not. Exhaustion of resources is the consequence of tunneling, of single-minded seeking, of a disequilibrium between need and object. The casual encounter is a grace note; gift rather than sustenance.

What do you do? You work so hard!

For a compulsive (and we are, by and large, a nation of compulsives or we wouldn't be a nation on tranquilizers), the move to the country is difficult. Old houses and nature itself conspire against the orderly life. If the number of one's entertainments and escapes are dramatically reduced, the field for one's labors is greatly enlarged.

And I do mean one's *own* labors; since the service economy has not yet arrived in small-town America, you do
for yourself or you wait. If the unfinished is abhorrent,
if disorder is difficult to bear, if the unpredictable is
upsetting, and if doing it yourself is a last and unloved
resort, then you had better think twice about moving to
the country.

A farm is particularly trying for the former urban/
suburbanite. Until you actually live on a farm you tend
to think of it in terms of scenery, with the livestock
provided by central casting. In reality, to live on a farm
is to become president of a small, impoverished, third-
world nation, which in addition to everything else requires fencing. The work is endless. That doesn't mean,
as in common usage, that there is an awful lot of it. It
means that it is endless. Without end. Forever and ever.
No amen.

For every day spent sitting on a tractor under a warm
June sun, captain of all you survey, there are probably
two spent repairing the damn thing. For every sunset
walk around the garden, hand in hand, admiring the
peas, there is an entire morning spent locked in hand-to-
hand combat with the bindweed. For every fence post
replaced, another is rotting; for every path of erosion
stopped, another is beginning. But gradually, with the
clues provided by sunrise and sunset, by the creatures of
the fields and the birds of the air, by green and growing
things, and by your neighbors (whose visits ought to tell
you something) you begin to realize that if it doesn't get
done today it will get done tomorrow, and that if it
doesn't get done tomorrow, what of it? Life will go on.
And meanwhile, it is *good*.